3rd Workshop on Semantic Web and Information Extraction

(SWAIE 2014)

Held at COLING 2014

Dublin, Ireland
24 August 2014

ISBN: 978-1-63439-229-7

Printed from e-media with permission by:

Curran Associates, Inc.
57 Morehouse Lane
Red Hook, NY 12571

proceedings.com

Some format issues inherent in the e-media version may also appear in this print version.

Printed by Curran Associates, Inc. (2014)

Association for Computational Linguistics
209 N. Eighth Street
Stroudsburg, Pennsylvania 18360

Phone: 1-570-476-8006
Fax: 1-570-476-0860

acl@aclweb.org

Additional copies of this publication are available from:

Curran Associates, Inc.
57 Morehouse Lane
Red Hook, NY 12571 USA
Phone: 845-758-0400
Fax: 845-758-2634
Email: curran@proceedings.com
Web: www.proceedings.com

Introduction

There is a vast wealth of information available in textual format that the Semantic Web cannot yet tap into: 80% of data on the Web and on internal corporate intranets is unstructured, hence analysing and structuring the data – social analytics and next generation analytics – is a large and growing endeavour. Here, the Information Extraction community could help as they specialise in mining the nuggets of information from text. Information Extraction techniques could be enhanced by annotated data or domain-specific resources. The Semantic Web community has taken great strides in making these resources available through the Linked Open Data cloud, which are now ready for uptake by the Information Extraction community. Following the previous two SWAIE workshops at EKAW 2012 and RANLP 2013 respectively, we have focused our attention on fostering awareness of how Semantic Web technologies can benefit the traditional IE and NLP communities.

The workshop invited contributions around three particular topics: 1) Semantic Web-driven Information Extraction, 2) Information Extraction for the Semantic Web, and 3) applications and architectures on the intersection of Semantic Web and Information Extraction SWAIE 2014 had a number of high-quality submissions. From these, 6 high quality papers were selected.

Two keynote speakers were invited to the workshop. The first talk was provided by D.J. McCloskey, NLP Architect in IBM's Watson Solutions division. The keynote presented the post-Watson role of Information Extraction and its intersection with the Multilingual Semantic Web. The second talk was provided by Lorraine Goeuriot, CNGL, DCU on Ontology Based IE for the medical domain. We would like to thank the many people who helped make SWAIE 2014 such a success: the Programme Committee, the paper contributors, the invited speakers and all the participants present at the workshop who engaged in lively debate.

Diana Maynard, University of Sheffield
Marieke van Erp, VU University Amsterdam
Brian Davis, INSIGHT@NUI Galway

Organizers:

Diana Maynard, University of Sheffield
Marieke van Erp, VU University Amsterdam
Brian Davis, INSIGHT@NUI Galway

Program Committee:

Eneko Agirre, University of the Basque Country, Spain
Paul Buitelaar, INSIGHT@ NUIGalway, Ireland
Elena Cabrio, INRIA Sophia Antipolis Méditerannée, France
Philipp Cimiano,CITEC University of Bielefeld, Germany
Hamish Cunningham, University of Sheffield, UK
Mariana Damova, Mozajka, Bulgaria
Dana Dannélls, University of Gothenburg, Sweden
Thierry DeClerck, DFKI, Germany
Antske Fokkens, VU University Amsterdam, the Netherlands
Jens Grivolla, Universitat Pompeu Fabra, Spain
Dirk Hovy, University of Copenhagen, Denmark
Phil Gooch, City University London, UK
Siegfried Handschuh, INSIGHT@ NUIGalway, Ireland
John Judge, CNGL Dublin City University, Ireland
David Lewis, CNGL Trinity College Dublin, Ireland
Alex O'Conor, CNGL Trinity College Dublin, Ireland
Laurette Pretorius, University of South Africa, South Africa
Birgit Proell, Johannes Kepler University Linz, Austria
German Rigau, University of the Basque Country, Spain
Marco Rospocher, Fondazione Bruno Kessler, Italy
Sara Tonelli,Fondazione Bruno Kessler, Italy

Invited Speaker:

D.J. McCloskey, IBM Watson Solutions, Dublin
Lorraine Goeuriot, CNGL, Dublin

Table of Contents

Workshop Program

Corpus-based Translation of Ontologies for Improved Multilingual Semantic Annotation
Claudia Bretschneider, Heiner Oberkampf, Sonja Zillner, Bernhard Bauer and Matthias Hammon

Information Extraction for Social Media
Mena Badieh Habib Morgan and Maurice van Keulen

Seed Selection for Distantly Supervised Web-Based Relation Extraction
Isabelle Augenstein

Ontology-based Extraction of Structured Information from Publications on Preclinical Experiments for Spinal Cord Injury Treatments
Benjamin Paassen, Andreas Stöckel, Raphael Dickfelder, Jan Philip Göpfert, Nicole Brazda, Tarek Kirchhoffer, Hans Werner Müller, Roman Klinger, Matthias Hartung and Philipp Cimiano

Semi-supervised Sequence Labeling for Named Entity Extraction based on Tri-Training: Case Study on Chinese Person Name Extraction
Chien-Lung Chou, Chia-Hui Chang and Shin-Yi Wu

Towards a robust framework for the semantic representation of temporal expressions in cultural legacy data
Daniel Isemann, Gerard Lynch and Raffaella Lanino

Corpus-based Translation of Ontologies for Improved Multilingual Semantic Annotation

Claudia Bretschneider[1,2], Heiner Oberkampf[1,3], Sonja Zillner[1], Bernhard Bauer[3], Matthias Hammon[4]
[1]Siemens AG, Corporate Technology, Munich, Germany
[2]Center for Information and Language Processing, University Munich, Germany
[3]Software Methodologies for Distributed Systems, University Augsburg, Germany
[4]Department of Radiology, University Hospital Erlangen, Germany
{claudia.bretschneider.ext,heiner.oberkampf.ext,sonja.zillner}@siemens.com,
bernhard.bauer@informatik.uni-augsburg.de, matthias.hammon@uk-erlangen.de

Abstract

Ontologies have proven to be useful to enhance NLP-based applications such as information extraction. In the biomedical domain rich ontologies are available and used for semantic annotation of texts. However, most of them have either no or only few non-English concept labels and cannot be used to annotate non-English texts. Since translations need expert review, a full translation of large ontologies is often not feasible. For semantic annotation purpose, we propose to use the corpus to be annotated to identify high occurrence terms and their translations to extend respective ontology concepts. Using our approach, the translation of a subset of ontology concepts is sufficient to significantly enhance annotation coverage. For evaluation, we automatically translated RadLex ontology concepts from English into German. We show that by translating a rather small set of concepts (in our case 433), which were identified by corpus analysis, we are able to enhance the amount of annotated words from 27.36 % to 42.65 %.

1 Introduction

Ontologies offer a powerful way to represent a shared understanding of a conceptualization of a domain (Gruber, 1993a). They define concepts and relations between them. Further linguistic information, such as labels, synonyms, abbreviations or definitions, can be attached. This is how ontologies provide a controlled vocabulary for the respective domain. In Information Extraction (IE), the controlled vocabulary of ontologies is used to recognize ontology concepts in text (also referred to as *semantic annotation*) and combine the textual information and the ontological knowledge to allow a deeper understanding of the text's semantics.

The problem, however, is that most of the available ontologies are not multilingual, i.e., they have either no or only few non-English concept labels. To make ontologies applicable for IE-based applications dealing with non-English texts, one has to translate at least some of the concept labels. Since high quality translations need expert review, a full translation of big ontologies is often not feasible. In the biomedical domain, ontologies have a long tradition and many well designed, large and semantically rich ontologies exist. At the time of writing, the BioPortal (Noy et al., 2008), an ontology repository for the biomedical domain, contains 370 ontologies, where 49 have more than 10,000 concepts. Their complete translation would be very costly.

In many application scenarios, only a subset of ontology concepts is of relevance. This is especially true for IE: If we consider, e.g., the semantic annotation of medical records in the context of a specific disease, the translation of a subset of ontology concept labels can be sufficient to increase the number of ontology concepts found. Thus, the translation of a small set of labels, which is relevant for the application scenario, is sufficient to increase the ontology's applicability for IE from non-English texts.

That is why we propose a translation approach that identifies the *most relevant concepts* for the application scenario and adds their translations to the ontology. The application scenario is represented by the *corpus*, a 'large set of domain-specific text'. In the context of IE, the main goal is to achieve a

Proceedings of Third Workshop on Semantic Web and Information Extraction, pages 1–8,
Dublin, Ireland, 24 August, 2014.

high annotation coverage, i.e., a high amount of words are semantically annotated with the correlating ontology concepts. Therefore, we define the terms with *high frequency* in the corpus as *most relevant* for translation, as the translation of high frequency terms increases the annotation coverage significantly. To demonstrate the feasibility of our approach, we use the RadLex ontology (Langlotz, 2006) and a corpus of German radiology reports of lymphoma patients.

2 Related Work

Ontology-based IE is a commonly used technique in the biomedical domain. (Meystre et al., 2008) give a detailed overview of recent research activities. However, most projects focus on English texts. The ontology translation problem was first described by (Gruber, 1993b) and further formalized by (Espinoza et al., 2009b). The subproblem we are dealing with is ontology localization, which (Suárez-figueroa and Gómez-Pérez, 2008) refers to as 'the adaptation of an ontology to a particular language and culture'. The challenges of ontology localization are analyzed in (Espinoza et al., 2009b) and a general methodology for guiding the localization process is presented. By (Cimiano et al., 2010), ontology localization can affect two different layers: the lexical layer (labels, definitions and accompanying documentation in natural language) and the conceptualization itself. Thus, the translation of concept labels we conduct can be seen as a subtask of ontology localization targeting only the lexical layer. The focus of our work does not lie in the machine translation task itself but in the intelligent use of existing resources for multilingual extension of ontologies with the aim to enhance the annotation coverage for a certain corpus. (Espinoza et al., 2009a) focus on sense disambiguation as major problem in ontology localization, while we investigate how to increase the efficiency by incorporating a corpus.

3 Overview of the approach

As explained, our main goal is to enhance the annotation coverage of a given non-English corpus by ontology translation. Using the corpus to be annotated within the translation process has three advantages:

- The translation is conducted more efficiently, since we reduce the number of translations that require a review. This is because only concepts that actually occur in the corpus are proposed as translations.
- The process results in high quality translations, because the corpus can be used to disambiguate the correct (target) translation candidate for a concept automatically.
- By facilitating a corpus, we make sure that the terms extracted as (target) translation candidates result in semantic text annotations in the end.

Figure 1 illustrates the approach: Based on the corpus information, "Läsion" is added as German translation to the ontology concept with RID38780. Now, the corpus term can be annotated, which was not possible before.

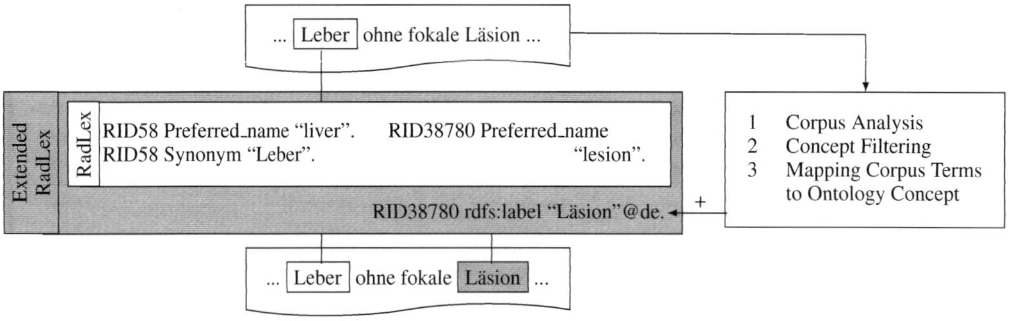

Figure 1: The text *Leber ohne fokale Läsion* "Liver without focal lesion" from a large medical corpus is processed and a new translation is added to the ontology to increase the number of semantic annotations.

The system designed makes use of this rationale and implements an approach that operates in three steps (as illustrated in Figure 2) for translating the ontology vocabulary:

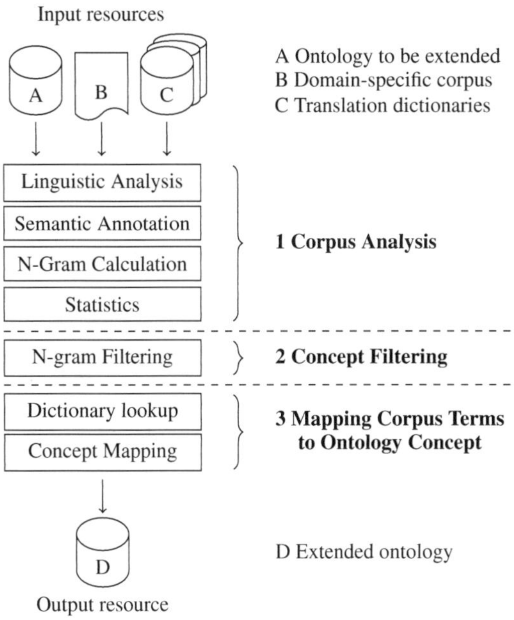

Figure 2: Processing steps in text analysis system

```
@prefix rdfs:
  <http://www.w3.org/2000/01/rdf-schema#> .
@prefix radlex:
  <http://www.owl-ontologies.com/
  Ontology1375951364.owl#> .

radlex:RID58
  rdfs:subClassOf radlex:RID13419 ;
  radlex:Preferred_name "liver"^^xsd:string ;
  radlex:Synonym "Leber"^^xsd:string ;

radlex:RID38780
  rdfs:subClassOf radlex:RID34300 ;
  radlex:Preferred_name "lesion"^^xsd:string ;
  rdfs:label "Läsion"@de.
```

Figure 3: (Incomplete) RDF representation of the RadLex concept radlex:RID58 with German translation 'Leber' as currently maintained as radlex:Synonym and concept radlex:RID38780 with translation 'Läsion' and proposed representation using rdfs:label and language tags

1 Corpus Analysis The initial processing step is designed to make use of the corpus to find the high frequency terms. Using this resource allows us to customize our approach for the required application scenario. Its content is used to digest the most relevant concepts for translation and determine the correct translation option. The processing incorporates linguistic and statistical NLP techniques to extract terms in target language with high frequency from the corpus.

2 Concept Filtering As the list of extracted terms still includes terms without semantic importance, we introduce this step in order to reduce the list. This includes the removal of terms with certain technical characters but also those with special linguistic structures, which makes the approach more efficient.

3 Mapping Corpus Terms to Ontology Concepts Our approach is targeted to translate only existing ontology concepts. Thus, we need a mechanism to map the terms of the corpus to the ontology concepts. We do this by employing state-of-the-art dictionary lookups: The English dictionary equivalences of the German corpus terms are used to find ontology concepts with the same English labels. Then, the (corpus) term is added as translation to the matching ontology concept as non-English label. The resulting translated ontology can be used in subsequent NLP-based applications and is able to serve the need for non-English texts.

In the end, the ontology will be extended with translations. In our case, the RadLex ontology currently maintains translations as synonyms, but we propose the usage of rdfs:label and language tags as shown in Figure 3. The introduced steps are described in detail in the following sections.

4 Corpus-Based Analysis and Concept Filtering

4.1 Corpus Description

One of the core resources for the approach is a domain-specific corpus. Combined with the ontology to be translated it serves several purposes: On the one hand, based on IE techniques we find and extract translations from the corpus in order to extend the ontology's vocabulary. Further, we use the corpus as semantic annotation target, which is annotated with ontology terms. The language-specific translations used for semantic annotation were found before with the help of the corpus itself. For the study, we use a corpus of 2,713 radiology reports (from 27 different readers[1]) of lymphoma patients containing the findings and evaluation sections.

4.2 Linguistic Analysis

This initial analysis includes several steps that enable a statistical analysis of the textual context. Each of the processing steps is implemented as a single UIMA annotator and integrated into an overall pipeline.

First, semantic information units such as dates and measurements are recognized using regular expressions. Medical language is rich in abbreviations. Particularly radiologists make use of them, because they allow an efficient reporting. Therefore, as second step, we build an abbreviation recognition and extension algorithm on a simple dictionary. The third linguistic task is the determination of the basic processing units: (1) tokens and (2) sentences. Tokens are split employing the spaces and '-' in the text, hence no compound splitting is conducted. While token splitting is a rather simple task, sentence splitting requires disambiguation facilities. Indicators like '?','!',';','.' are used to determine sentence ends. However, the full stop determines sentence ends only if they are not part of a measurement, date or abbreviation. As a fourth step, stopwords are removed from the documents to reduce the content to only relevant tokens. Available language-dependent stopword lists are employed. Finally, each of the tokens in the text is stemmed with the German version of the Porter stemmer. (Porter, 1997)

4.3 Semantic Annotation

Since most ontologies are already *partially* translated, we make use of this fact and semantically annotate concepts and exclude them in the subsequent filter process (Section 4.6). The annotator implementation is based on the UIMA ConceptMapper (Tanenblatt et al., 2010). The annotation dictionary is built from the preferred names and synonyms in the RadLex ontology (as shown in Figure 3). Our concept mapper combines the stems of the dictionary terminology and the stems of the text tokens and annotates the matches with the ontology information. If a dictionary term consists of more than one token, an annotation is created if all of its stems are contained in a single sentence of the corpus. That is also how single tokens can be assigned more than one annotation.

4.4 N-Gram Calculation

After the linguistic processing of the preceding steps, the actual term extraction can be performed. In this initial work, we limit the length of n-grams to three because of performance reasons. Furthermore, we define that the individual tokens of an n-gram have to co-occur within the same sentence. The output of this step is a list of terms in target language that are candidates for ontology translation.

4.5 Statistics

The n-grams relevant for translation are determined by their frequency in the corpus. Based on the stems, the frequency of each n-gram is calculated according to their (co-)occurrence. The individual (co-)occurrence count of the terms is used for ordering of the terms, whereas the most frequent occurring term is ranked top.

4.6 N-Gram Filtering

The list of high frequency terms still contains several terms with tokens representing special characters and sentence ends (like '.', '?', '<', '>', '/') or semantic classes meaningless for ontology extension (like dates, measurements, negation, and image references). Since the overall aim is to identify concepts that should be added as translations to the ontology, we remove occurrences of these information units that are very specific and without ontology importance. Also, if the term contains numbers, this precise and

[1] In the radiology domain, readers are physicians, who read and interpret radiology images and produce the reports analyzed in this work.

rather technical information is removed from the n-gram list. The resulting list contains terms we would like to add as labels to respective ontology concepts if available.

5 Mapping Corpus Terms to Ontology Concepts

Based on the list of terms ranked by their frequency, we identify ontology concepts, whose translations have a high impact on annotation coverage for the respective corpus. We assume that each ontology concept has at least one label in the source language, in our case in English. In the following, we describe our language resources employed in the approach and the mapping procedure.

5.1 Translation dictionaries

For this work, we used German-English translations from Dict.cc[2] and multilingual information from DBpedia to create two dictionaries.

1. **Medical Dictionary: 60,082 different English entries**
   Dict.cc contains specialized dictionaries for 130 different subjects. For our medical dictionary, we collected all entries from the specialized dictionaries with subjects 'anatomy', 'biology', 'chemistry', 'medicine', 'pharmacy', and 'medical engineering and imaging'. Additionally, we retrieved all medically relevant concepts from DBpedia that have an English and a German or Latin label (about 9,500 concepts). More precisely, we used the DBpedia ontology (Bizer et al., 2009) to retrieve all concepts of type dbp:AnatomicalStructure[3], dbp:Disease, dbp:Drug, dbp:ChemicalSubstance and subclasses (see SPARQL query in Figure 4).

2. **General Dictionary: 623,294 different English entries**
   The general dictionary is the complete English-German Dict.cc dictionary without restriction to a specific subject.

```
PREFIX rdfs:      <http://www.w3.org/2000/01/rdf-schema#>
PREFIX dbp:       <http://dbpedia.org/ontology/>
PREFIX dbpedia2:  <http://dbpedia.org/property/>
SELECT ?s ?labelEn ?labelDe ?labelLat
WHERE {
    ?s a ?type ;
       rdfs:label ?labelEn .
    FILTER ( ?type = dbp:AnatomicalStructure
        || ?type = dbp:Disease
        || ?type = dbp:Drug
        || ?type = dbp:ChemicalSubstance )
    FILTER ( lang(?labelEn) = "en" )
    OPTIONAL { ?s dbpedia2:latin ?labelLat }
    OPTIONAL { ?s rdfs:label ?labelDe .
        FILTER ( lang(?labelDe) = "de" ) }
    FILTER( bound(?labelDe) || bound(?labelLat) )
}
```

Figure 4: SPARQL query to retrieve English-German and English-Latin translations from DBpedia using the SPARQL endpoint at http://dbpedia.org/sparql.

5.2 Ontology concept translation

The mapping of given corpus terms to corresponding ontology concepts as translations involves two sub steps.

1. **Dictionary Lookup** For all occurrences of a term, we try to find English options in our dictionaries. If no complete lookup option is found for a n-gram, we try to find a lookup option in the dictionary for each single token to combine them into a complete English n-gram. E.g. the corpus term "Läsion" is translated to "lesion" using the medical dictionary.

[2] http://www.dict.cc/
[3] We use the prefix notation dbp for http://dbpedia.org/ontology/AnatomicalStructure

2. **Concept Mapping** The list of English lookup options from the first step is used to find ontology concepts, whose (English) labels match the dictionary lookup. We find that the ontology concept with RID38780 is assigned the given preferred name "lesion". If a match is found, the German n-gram that resulted in the match ("Läsion") is regarded as probable translation. In order to increase the quality of the translation, an expert review is conducted at this time. This is the only manual step in the whole translation process. After the review, the n-gram is inserted as new RDF triple for the respective ontology concept. In RadLex translations are currently maintained as synonyms. However, as this modeling of translations as synonyms does not represent the correct semantics and misses the important language information, we propose to use rdfs:label for translations added by a corresponding language tag. Thus, for the example we insert "Läsion" as additional German label to the ontology concept (see Figure 3).

6 Evaluation

6.1 Resources

The evaluation of our system is based on the RadLex ontology and a corpus of 2,713 radiology reports of lymphoma patients. We use the OWL DL version of RadLex3.9.1 from NCBO BioPortal. This version contains 42,321 concepts, which all have an assigned (English) preferred name and few additionally synonyms. The German translations are represented as synonyms. Most of the German labels were added in 2009, when a first German version was created. Even though the number of concepts is growing significantly (RadLex3.9 contained 34,899), the number of concepts with non-English labels is not evolving the same way. Thus, in RadLex3.9.1 less than 25% of the 42,321 concepts have German labels.

Proposed translations for ontology concepts - as output of the described automatic approach - are evaluated by a clinical expert. We restricted the corpus terms translated to those occurring at least two times. The whole process results in a list of 742 German labels proposed for ontology extension. The expert classified these translations as correct or incorrect. In order to assist the expert in better understanding of the ontology concept to be extended, we provide information on the preferred name, synonyms as well as preferred names of the next two super classes.

This list of evaluated translations is analyzed in detail using three dimensions: First, we analyze how the choice of the dictionary influences the translation outcome. Second, we figure out how the term length and the processing of multi-word terms influences the translation results. Third, the correct translations are added to an extended RadLex ontology. We compare the annotation results using the initial and extended RadLex version. We apply *accuracy* as evaluation measure, which is the proportion of correct translations in the system-proposed set.

6.2 Evaluation of the Translation Services

As described in Section 5.1, we use two different dictionaries. As expected, the accuracy of the medical dictionary is significantly higher than the accuracy of the general dictionary (see Table 1(a)). This is because in many cases only the domain-specific dictionary contains the correct lookup entry for the terms. Nevertheless, the general dictionary is necessary, because RadLex contains also general language terms like 'increased' or 'normal'. Combining the two dictionaries accuracy reaches 75.2%.

6.3 Evaluation of the N-Gram Length

If we take a closer look at n-gram distribution of terms, we see that we translate mainly single words (1-grams), while 2-grams and 3-grams are translated less often. However, the accuracy of 3-grams reaches excellent values (see Table 1(b)). Nevertheless, the translation of n-grams is of high importance, as most of the ontology concepts in the biomedical domain have multiword labels. In particular, labels of anatomical entities are multiword terms; in RadLex they can grow to 10-grams. Consider for example 'Organ component of lymphatic tree organ' or 'Tendon of second palmar interosseous of left hand'.

Thus, a more sophisticated multiword translation is needed to enhance the number of translations for n-grams. For us, the improved handling of stopwords is the main focus in future work: While we remove stopwords in the n-grams, ontology concepts that contain stopwords prevent a match.

Table 1: Evaluation of translation outcomes by choice of dictionary and term length. *Proposed* denotes the number of German labels translated and added to the ontology. *Correct* denotes the subset of translations evaluated by the expert as correct.

(a) Evaluation by translation dictionary

	Translations		
	Proposed	**Correct**	**Accuracy**
medical dict	258	240	0.9302
general dict	484	318	0.6570
both dicts	742	558	0.7520

(b) Evaluation by n-gram length

	Translations		
	Proposed	**Correct**	**Accuracy**
1-grams	609	451	0.7406
2-grams	118	92	0.7797
3-grams	15	15	1.0000

Table 2: Comparison of the annotation coverage using RadLex3.9.1 and the extended version. Total number of tokens of the corpus: 346,963.

	RadLex3.9.1	**extended RadLex3.9.1**	
Tokens with annotation	94,914	147,982	+0.5591
Annotation Coverage	27.36 %	42.65 %	+0.5591
Tokens without annotation	252,049	198,981	- 0.2105
Number of annotations	133,156	204,491	+0.5357

6.4 Extension of RadLex and Evaluation of Annotation Coverage

From Table 1(a), one can see that we correctly translated 558 RadLex concept labels using both dictionaries. After the expert review, we added the (German) terms of these correct matches as labels to 433 distinct RadLex concepts. I.e., some concepts were assigned more than one additional German label. We refer to the new ontology as the *extended RadLex*. For the analysis of how the added translations influence the number of annotations, we conducted two annotation processes. Both the original and the extended RadLex versions were used to semantically annotate the corpus using the annotator described in Section 4.3. The measure to indicate the annotation success is *annotation coverage*, which denotes the relative amount of tokens for which at least one annotation exists. Table 2 shows that we are able to enhance the annotation coverage by about 56% by adding only 558 translations. This shows the effectiveness of the approach. A comparison indicator of these numbers deliver English texts: In (Woods and Eng, 2013) an annotation rate of 62 % was observed for English chest radiography reports. Despite the restrictiveness of the comparison, we see that an annotation coverage of 42.65 % is high considering that only about 25 % of the extended RadLex's concepts have a German label.

6.5 Limitations

Due to the characteristics of our approach, the outcome of the increased annotation coverage is specific for the corpus used: Even though the reports come from 27 different readers, the vocabulary of the evaluated corpus is specific to one disease and thus limited to a certain degree. Because the vocabulary differentiates in other corpora, the application of the translation added for texts describing other diseases or reports may not result in increases of the annotation coverage as shown. For other corpora, one has to run our approach a second time using the new corpus and add further concepts to obtain a similar annotation coverage. However, we expect the additional effort needed to get smaller over time.

7 Conclusion

We propose a method to make ontologies usable for multilingual semantic annotation of texts by automatically extending them with translations, without the need to invest much effort in a full translation. We believe that our approach is able to unlock the high potential of existing ontologies also for low resourced languages. We address the key problem of identifying those concepts that are worth translating by defining the increase of annotation coverage for a given corpus as the main target. Although it might seem intuitive to apply an English corpus to identify the most frequent terms and their (source) ontology concepts to translate, we do not pursue this approach. Especially when dealing with a domain-specific language, translations are often ambiguous. As the English corpus does not help picking the correct (target) translation candidate, we decided to start the other way around and facilitate a corpus in target language. We show the high quality and efficiency of the approach by translating medical terms from English to German. According to the evaluation results, a better treatment of n-grams shows the biggest potential for enhancement of the approach. Sophisticated linguistic algorithms for the translation, which incorporate the ontology context, can increase the matching of the multi-word terms. In future work, we plan to evaluate our approach using other ontologies from the BioPortal.

Acknowledgements

This research has been supported in part by the KDI project, which is funded by the German Federal Ministry of Economics and Technology under grant number 01MT14001. We thank Dict.cc for providing us with the dictionaries.

References

Christian Bizer, Jens Lehmann, Georgi Kobilarov, Sren Auer, Christian Becker, Richard Cyganiak, and Sebastian Hellmann. 2009. {DBpedia} - a crystallization point for the web of data. *Web Semantics: Science, Services and Agents on the World Wide Web*, 7(3):154 – 165.

Philipp Cimiano, Elena Montiel-Ponsoda, Paul Buitelaar, Mauricio Espinoza, and Asunción Gómez-Pérez. 2010. A note on ontology localization. *Applied Ontology*, 5(2):127–137.

M Espinoza, A Gómez-Pérez, and E Montiel-Ponsoda. 2009a. Multilingual and Localization Support for Ontologies. *The Semantic Web Research and Applications*, 5554:821–825.

Mauricio Espinoza, Elena Montiel-Ponsoda, and Asunción Gómez-Pérez. 2009b. Ontology localization. In *Proceedings of the Fifth International Conference on Knowledge Capture*, pages 33–40, New York. ACM.

Thomas R Gruber. 1993a. Toward Principles for the Design of Ontologies Used for Knowledge Sharing. *International Journal Human-Computer Studies 43*, pages 907–928.

Thomas R. Gruber. 1993b. A translation approach to portable ontology specifications. *Knowl. Acquis.*, 5(2):199–220, June.

Curtis P. Langlotz. 2006. Radlex: A new method for indexing online educational materials. *RadioGraphics*, 26(6):1595–1597. PMID: 17102038.

S.M. Meystre, G.K. Savova, K.C. Kipper-Schuler, and J.F. Hurdle. 2008. Extracting information from textual documents in the electronic health record: A review of recent research. *Yearbook of Medical Informatics*, pages 128–144.

Natalya F. Noy, Nigam H. Shah, Benjamin Dai, Michael Dorf, Nicholas Griffith, Clement Jonquet, Michael J. Montegut, Daniel L. Rubin, Cherie Youn, and Mark A. Musen. 2008. Bioportal: A web repository for biomedical ontologies and data resources [demonstration].

M. F. Porter. 1997. Readings in information retrieval. chapter An Algorithm for Suffix Stripping, pages 313–316. Morgan Kaufmann Publishers Inc., San Francisco, CA, USA.

Mari Carmen Suárez-figueroa and Asunción Gómez-Pérez. 2008. First Attempt towards a Standard Glossary of Ontology Engineering Terminology. In *Proceedings of the 8th International Conference on Terminology and Knowledge Engineering (TKE2008)*.

Michael Tanenblatt, Anni Coden, and Igor Sominsky. 2010. The conceptmapper approach to named entity recognition. In *Proceedings of the Seventh conference on International Language Resources and Evaluation (LREC'10)*, Valletta, Malta. European Language Resources Association (ELRA).

Ryan W. Woods and John Eng. 2013. Evaluating the Completeness of RadLex in the Chest Radiography Domain. *Academic Radiology*, 20(11):1329–1333.

Information Extraction for Social Media

Mena B. Habib
Chair Databases
University of Twente
m.b.habib@ewi.utwente.nl

Maurice van Keulen
Chair Databases
University of Twente
m.vankeulen@utwente.nl

Abstract

The rapid growth in IT in the last two decades has led to a growth in the amount of information available online. A new style for sharing information is social media. Social media is a continuously instantly updated source of information. In this position paper, we propose a framework for Information Extraction (IE) from unstructured user generated contents on social media. The framework proposes solutions to overcome the IE challenges in this domain such as the short context, the noisy sparse contents and the uncertain contents. To overcome the challenges facing IE from social media, State-Of-The-Art approaches need to be adapted to suit the nature of social media posts. The key components and aspects of our proposed framework are noisy text filtering, named entity extraction, named entity disambiguation, feedback loops, and uncertainty handling.

1 Introduction

The rapid growth in IT in the last two decades has led to a growth in the amount of information available on the World Wide Web. A new style for exchanging and sharing information is social media. Social media refers to the means of interaction among people in which they create, share, and exchange information and ideas in virtual communities and networks (like Twitter and Facebook). According to CNN[1], more Americans get their news from the Internet than from newspapers or radio, and three-fourths say they hear of news via e-mail or updates on social media sites. Social media, in many cases, provide more up-to-date information than conventional sources like online news. To make use of this vast amount of information, it is required to extract structured information out of these heterogeneous unstructured information. Information Extraction (IE) is the research field that enables the use of such a vast amount of unstructured distributed information in a structured way. IE systems analyse human language text in order to extract information about different types of events, entities, or relationships. Structured information could be stored in Knowledge-bases (KB) which hold facts and relations extracted from the free style text. A KB is an information repository that provides a means for information to be collected, organized, shared, searched and utilized. It can be either machine-readable or intended for human use.

In this paper, we introduce a framework for IE from unstructured user generated contents on social media. Although IE is a field of research that has been studied for long time, there is very few work done on that field for social media contents. (Bontcheva et al., 2013) proposed TwitIE, an open-source NLP pipeline customised to microblog text. However, TwitIE doesn't provide mechanisms for messages filtering or named entity disambiguation or relation/fact extraction. All efforts on IE field focus on facts extraction from encyclopaedias like Wikipedia (Suchanek et al., 2007; Auer and Lehmann, 2007), or from web pages (Nakashole et al., 2011; Carlson et al., 2010; Kushmerick et al., 1997; Crescenzi et al., 2001).

IE from text is an important task in text mining. The general goal of information extraction is to discover structured information from unstructured or semi-structured text. For example, given the tweets shown in figure 1, we can extract the following information:

[1]http://edition.cnn.com/2010/TECH/03/01/social.network.news/index.html

Proceedings of Third Workshop on Semantic Web and Information Extraction, pages 9–16,
Dublin, Ireland, 24 August, 2014.

(a) Example 1.

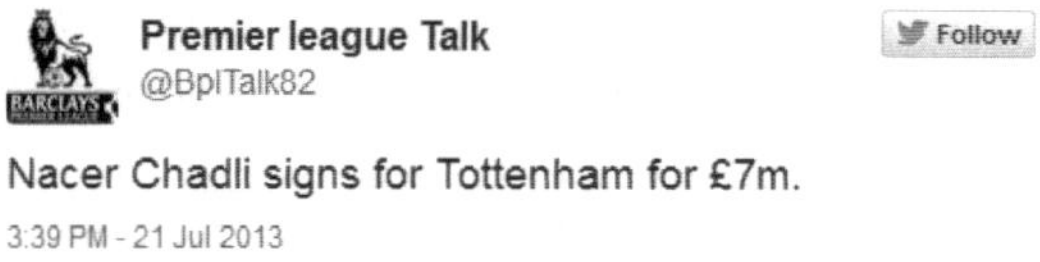

(b) Example 2.

(c) Example 3.

Figure 1: Tweets examples

Example (1):
`Called(U.S. state of Ohio, Buckeye State),`
`FoundedIn(The Ohio State University, 1870).`

Example (2):
`SignedFor(Nacer Chadli (the football player), Tottenham Hotspur Football Club).`

Example (3):
`Fire(1600 Belmont Avenue, Fort Worth, TX),`
`Fire(2900 Avenue G., Fort Worth, TX).`

As we can see in the examples, IE can be applied for open or closed domain. Open IE is to extract all possible relations and facts stated in a post as in examples 1 and 2. Closed domain IE is to extract facts for a specific target domain or fill in predefined templates like example 3. Other meta data could be extracted like the time or the source of the extracted fact. This could help in improving the precision of the extraction process. For instance, in the 3rd example, it is not stated where exactly is the "`1600 Belmont Avenue`" or "`2900 Avenue G.`". We could infer this extra knowledge from the source of the tweet "`Fort Worth Fire Dept`". Same with example 2, the word "`Tottenham`" is ambiguous. Further information about the entity "`Nacer Chadli`" should help to link "`Tottenham`" to "`Tottenham Hotspur Football Club`".

2 Challenges

Application of the State-Of-The-Art approaches on social media is not reasonable for the following challenges:

- **Informal language:** Posted texts are noisy and written in an informal setting, include misspellings, lack punctuation and capitalisation, use non-standard abbreviations, and do not contain grammatically correct sentences. Traditional KB construction approaches rely mostly on capitalization and

Part-Of-Speech tags to extract the named entities. The lack of such features in social media posts makes the IE task more challenging.

- **Short context:** There is a post length limit on some social media networks like Twitter. This limit forces the users to use more abbreviations to express more information in their posts. The shortness of the posts makes it more challenging to disambiguate mentioned entities and to resolve co-references among tweets.

- **Noisy sparse contents:** The users' posts on social media are not always important nor contain useful information. Around 40% of twitter messages content are pointless babble[2]. Filtering is a pre-processing step that is required to purify the input posts stream.

- **Information about non-famous entities:** The IE State-Of-The-Art approaches link the entities involved in the extracted information to a KB. However, people normally use social media to express information about themselves or about some small local events (street festival or accident) and thus the involved entities are not contained in a KB. New ways of entity linkage need to be introduced to suit IE from social media posts.

- **Uncertain contents:** Of course not every available information is trustworthy. In addition to errors that may take place during the IE process, information contained in users' contributions is often partial, subject to evolution over time, in conflict with other sources, and sometimes untrustworthy. It is required to handle the uncertainty involved in the extracted facts.

3 The State-Of-The-Art

In order to extract information from text, a set of subtasks has to be applied on the input text. Figure 2 shows the subtasks modules of a traditional IE system. Those modules are described according to the State-Of-The-Art IE approaches as follows:

- **Named Entity Extraction:** A named entity is a sequence of words that designates some real world entity (e.g. "California", "Steve Jobs" and "Apple Inc."). The task of named entity extraction (NEE), is to identify named entities from free-form text. This task cannot be simply accomplished by string matching against pre-compiled gazetteers because named entities of a given entity type usually do not form a closed set and therefore any gazetteer would be incomplete. NEE approaches mainly use capitalization features and Part-Of-Speech tags for recognizing named entities. Part-Of-Speech (POS) tagging is the process of marking up a word in a text (corpus) as corresponding to a particular Part-Of-Speech, based on both its definition, as well as its context (i.e. relationship with adjacent and related words in a phrase, sentence, or paragraph). A simplified form of this is commonly taught to school-age children, in the identification of words as nouns, verbs, adjectives, adverbs, etc.

- **Named Entity Disambiguation:** In natural language processing, named entity disambiguation (NED) or entity linking is the task of determining the identity of entities mentioned in text. For example, to link the mention "California" to the Wikipedia article "`http://en.wikipedia.org/wiki/California`". It is distinct from named entity extraction (NEE) in that it identifies not the occurrence of names but their reference. NED needs a KB of entities to which names can be linked. A popular choice for entity linking on open domain text is Wikipedia (Cucerzan, 2007; Hoffart et al., 2011).

- **Fact Extraction:** In open IE, the goal of the fact extraction (FE) module is to detect and characterize the semantic relations between entities in text or relations between entities and values. In closed domain IE, the goal is to fill in a predefined template using the extracted named entities.

[2] `http://web.archive.org/web/20110715062407/www.pearanalytics.com/blog/wp-content/uploads/2010/05/Twitter-Study-August-2009.pdf`

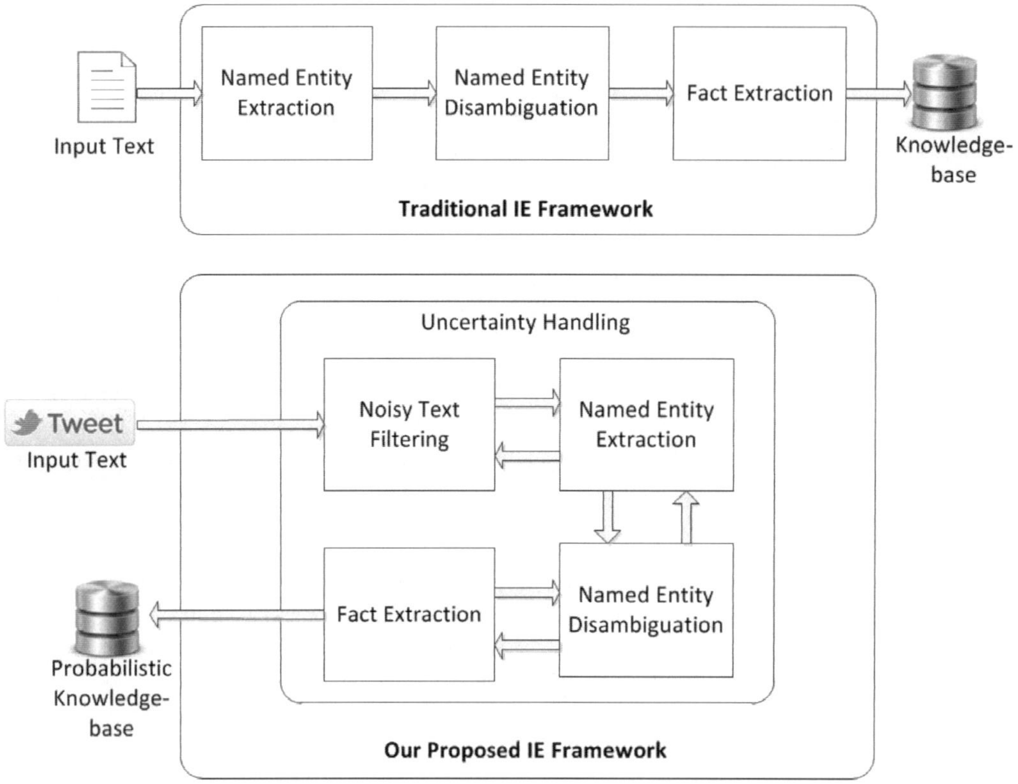

Figure 2: Traditional IE framework versus our proposed IE framework.

4 Proposed Framework

To overcome the challenges facing IE from social media, State-Of-The-Art approaches need to be adapted to suit the nature of social media posts. Here, we describe the key components and aspects of our proposed framework (see figure 2) and show how it would overcome the challenges.

- **Noisy Text Filtering:** There are millions of social media posts every day. For example, the average number of tweets exceeds 140 million tweet per day sent by over 200 million users around the world. These numbers are growing exponentially[3]. This huge number of posts not always contains useful information about users, locations, events, etc. It is required to filter non-informative posts. Filtering could be done based on domain or language or other criteria to make sure to keep only relevant posts that contains information about the domain need to be processed. For example, if we want to extract the results of all the football World Cup matches from tweets, we need to filter millions of tweets to get only the subset of tweets that contain information about results of matches, note that even this subset may contains predicted results or results changing during the matches.

- **Named Entity Extraction:** With the lack of formal writing style, we need new approaches for NEE that don't rely heavily on syntactic features like capitalization and POS. In (Habib et al., 2013), we participated in a challenge to extract named entities from microposts of tweets, we proposed a new approach that combines State-Of-The-Art techniques with clues derived from disambiguation step to detect named entities. Our system named to be the best among all the challenge participants (Basave et al., 2013).

- **Named Entity Disambiguation:** As stated in the State-Of-The-Art section, researchers normally link entities to Wikipedia articles or to KB entries. For social media posts, sometimes this is not

[3] `http://www.marketinggum.com/twitter-statistics-2011-updated-stats/`

FCT still 1 - 0 up after 35min. Moroole and Muller breaking up every Ajax attack

7:08 PM - 7 Dec 2012

(a) Example 4.

FC Tygerberg vs Ajax Cape Town Goals: youtu.be/wo6qpYKvs_g

9:42 AM - 9 Dec 2012

(b) Example 5.

Figure 3: Tweets examples

possible as many of the mentioned entities cannot be linked to Wikipedia articles or a KB entries. However, normally users have home pages or profiles on a social media network. Furthermore, festivals and local events also commonly have home pages representing these events. In (Habib and van Keulen, 2013), we proposed an open world approach for NED for tweets. Named entities are disambiguated by linking them to a home page or a social network profile page in case they don't have a Wikipedia article. Target tweets (tweets revolving around same event) are used to enrich the tweet context and hence to improve the effectiveness of finding the correct entity page. Other meta data from users profiles could also be used to improve the disambiguation process.

- **Feedback Loops:** In figure 2, we can see, in the traditional IE framework, the pipeline of the subtasks. Each subtask processes the input and generates an output and passes this output to the next subtask. There is no possibility of modifying or refining the output of one subtask once it is already generated. In our framework, feedback plays a key role in the system. Every subtask gives a feedback to the preceding subtask which allows for possibility of iterations of refinement (Habib and van Keulen, 2012). For example, if the NEE module extracted the mention "Apple". And when NED module tries to disambiguate the extracted mention, it finds that it could not be linked to any entity. This means that most probably this mention "Apple" refers to the fruit rather than the company. In traditional approaches, such feedback cannot be passed, and the NED has to find a page to link the extracted mention anyway. Furthermore, as "Apple" is not considered a named entity anymore this may affect the decision made that this piece of text in non-informative and thus should be filtered. This is typically how human beings interpret text. In (Habib et al., 2014), we applied the proposed feedback loop on the #Microposts 2014 Named Entity Extraction and Linking Challenge. Our system is ranked second among all the challenge participants (Cano Basave et al., 2014).

  Similarly, the feedback loop takes place between the FE and the NED modules. This feedback helps resolving errors that took place earlier in the disambiguation step. For example in figure 3a, one might interpret that the tweet refers to a match of "FC Twente" versus "Ajax Amsterdam" in the Dutch football league. Unfortunately, this turns to be a wrong assumption after checking the tweet in figure 3b which shows that the match was between "FC Tygerberg" and "Ajax Cape Town" in the South African second division football league. A feedback from the FE module should trigger and correct the wrong decision made earlier in the NED module. It is also possible that the FE module sends a feedback message to the noisy text filtering module that the message is non-informative if it failed to extract the required information or if the extracted fact contradicts other facts or rules. For example, if we want to extract facts about the football World Cup, and we found a tweet the contains a fact about football club (not national team) then a feedback message is sent back to the noisy text filtering module to mark this tweet as irrelevant one.

- **Uncertainty Handling:** As mentioned in the challenges, the information contained in the social media posts involves high degree uncertainty due to many reason. We envision an approach that fundamentally treats annotations and extracted information as uncertain throughout the process.

(Goujon, 2009) models this uncertainty in a fuzzy way, however we believe that a probabilistic approach would be a better solution to handle such uncertainty. Probabilistic knowledge-bases (PKB) are KBs where each fact is associated with a probability indicating how trustworthy is this fact. Probabilities are updated according to many factors like time, users, contradiction or compatibility with other facts, etc.

Using the same example (figure 3a) mentioned above, the mention "FCT" is linked to "FC Twente" with some certainty confidence. This probability should be adjusted after processing the second tweet shown in figure 3b which holds a contradicting fact about the mention "FCT". Furthermore, a new fact is added to the KB indicating that "FCT" is linked to "FC Tygerberg". The benefit of using a PKB is that we can keep both interpretations "FC Twente" and "FC Tygerberg" with different probabilities assigned to them. Using a PKB, all information is preserved.

Another source of uncertainty is the knowledge updating. One true fact at certain point of time may be wrong at a later point of time. Scores of sport games change over time. Twitter users normally tweet about the score during and after the game. They may also write their predictions on the game prior to the game itself. A probabilistic model should be developed to handle those uncertainties using evidences like number of tweets with the same extracted result, number of re-tweets, time of the tweets, last extracted result about the game, etc.

- **Modules Portability:** Each module from our proposed framework could be customized and reused individually or embedded inside other frameworks. For example, NEE and NED modules could be used in a sentiment analysis system that measures the users opinions towards some product. Noisy text filtering could be embedded inside a search engine for social media posts.

5 Knowledge exchange and impact

The aim of this position paper is to propose a framework for information extraction from unstructured user generated contents on social media. IE systems analyse human language text in order to extract information about different types of events, entities, or relationships. Structured information could be stored in KB which hold facts and relations extracted from the free style text. A KB is a special kind of database for knowledge management. A KB is an information repository that provides a means for information to be collected, organized, shared, searched and utilized. Information extraction has applications in a wide range of domains. There is many stakeholders that would benefit from such framework. Here, we give some examples for applications of information extraction:

- Financial experts always look for specific information to help their decision making. Social media is a very important source of information about shareholders attitudes and behaviours. For example, a finance company may need to know the shareholders reaction towards some political action. Automatically finding such information from users posts on social media requires special information extraction technologies to analyse social media streams and capture such information at runtime.

- Security agencies normally analyse large amounts of text manually to search for information about people involved in criminal or terrorism activities. Social media is a continuously instantly updated source of information. Football hooligans sometimes start their fight electronically on social media networks even before the sport event. This information could be helpful to take actions to prevent such violent, and destructive behaviours.

- With the fast growth of the Web, search engines have become an integral part of people's daily lives, and users' search behaviours are much better understood now. Search based on bag-of-word representation of documents provides less satisfactory results for the new challenges and demands. More advanced search problems such as entity search, and question answering can provide users with better search experience. To facilitate these search capabilities, information extraction is often needed as a pre-processing step to enrich document representation or to populate an underlying database.

Our main goal of this proposal is to provide an open source set of portable and customizable modules that can be used by different stakeholders with different application needs on social media contents. Open source software is a computer software with its source code made available and licensed with a license in which the copyright holder provides the rights to study, change and distribute the software to anyone and for any purpose. This enables the ICT community from not only using but also developing and extending the system according to their needs. Individuals and organizations always choose open source software for their zero cost, and its adaptability.

Reusability would be a key feature in our framework design. In software industry, reusability is the likelihood that a part of a system can be used again to add new functionalities with slight or no modification. Reusable modules reduce implementation time and effort. As an example for possible contribution to the society, we contribute to the TEC4SE project [4]. The aim of the project is to improve the operational decision-making within the security domain by gathering as much information available from different sources (like cameras, police officers on field, or social media posts). Then these information is linked and relationships between different information streams are found. The result is a good overview of what is happening in the field of security in the region. Our contribution to this project to filter twitter stream messages and enrich it by extracting named entities at run time. It will be more valuable to this project to complete the whole IE process by building a complete KB from the extracted information for further or later investigations.

6 Conclusion

IE for social media is an emerging field of research. The noisy contents, shortness of posts, informality of used language, and the uncertainty involved, add more challenges to IE for social media over those of formal news articles. In this paper we propose a framework to cope with those challenges through set of portable modules. Messages filtering, feedback loops, and uncertainty handling are the key aspects of our framework.

References

Sören Auer and Jens Lehmann. 2007. What have innsbruck and leipzig in common? extracting semantics from wiki content. In *Proceedings of the 4th European Conference on The Semantic Web: Research and Applications*, ESWC '07, pages 503–517, Berlin, Heidelberg. Springer-Verlag.

Amparo E. Cano Basave, Matthew Rowe, Milan Stankovic, and Aba-Sah Dadzie, editors. 2013. *Proceedings, Concept Extraction Challenge at the 3rd Workshop on Making Sense of Microposts (#MSM2013): Big things come in small packages, Rio de Janeiro, Brazil, 13 May 2013*, May.

Kalina Bontcheva, Leon Derczynski, Adam Funk, Mark Greenwood, Diana Maynard, and Niraj Aswani. 2013. Twitie: An open-source information extraction pipeline for microblog text. In *In Proceedings of the International Conference on Recent Advances in Natural Language Processing. Association for Computational Linguistics.*

Amparo Elizabeth Cano Basave, Giuseppe Rizzo, Andrea Varga, Matthew Rowe, Milan Stankovic, and Aba-Sah Dadzie. 2014. Making sense of microposts (#microposts2014) named entity extraction & linking challenge. In *4th Workshop on Making Sense of Microposts (#Microposts2014)*, pages 54–60.

Andrew Carlson, Justin Betteridge, Richard C. Wang, Estevam R. Hruschka, Jr., and Tom M. Mitchell. 2010. Coupled semi-supervised learning for information extraction. In *Proceedings of the Third ACM International Conference on Web Search and Data Mining*, WSDM '10, pages 101–110, New York, NY, USA. ACM.

Valter Crescenzi, Giansalvatore Mecca, and Paolo Merialdo. 2001. Roadrunner: Towards automatic data extraction from large web sites. In *Proceedings of the 27th International Conference on Very Large Data Bases*, VLDB '01, pages 109–118, San Francisco, CA, USA. Morgan Kaufmann Publishers Inc.

Silviu Cucerzan. 2007. Large-scale named entity disambiguation based on Wikipedia data. In *Proceedings of the 2007 Joint Conference on Empirical Methods in Natural Language Processing and Computational Natural Language Learning (EMNLP-CoNLL)*, pages 708–716, Prague, Czech Republic, June. Association for Computational Linguistics.

[4] http://www.tec4se.nl/

Bénédicte Goujon. 2009. Uncertainty detection for information extraction. In *RANLP*, pages 118–122.

Mena B. Habib and Maurice van Keulen. 2012. Improving toponym disambiguation by iteratively enhancing certainty of extraction. In *Proceedings of the 4th International Conference on Knowledge Discovery and Information Retrieval, KDIR 2012, Barcelona, Spain*, pages 399–410, Spain, October. SciTePress.

Mena B. Habib and Maurice van Keulen. 2013. A generic open world named entity disambiguation approach for tweets. In *Proceedings of the 5th International Conference on Knowledge Discovery and Information Retrieval, KDIR 2013, Vilamoura, Portugal*, pages 267–276, Portugal, September. SciTePress.

Mena B. Habib, Maurice Van Keulen, and Zhemin Zhu. 2013. Concept extraction challenge: University of Twente at #msm2013. In Basave et al. (Basave et al., 2013), pages 17–20.

Mena B. Habib, Maurice van Keule, and Zhemin Zhu. 2014. Named entity extraction and linking challenge: University of twente at #microposts2014. In *4th Workshop on Making Sense of Microposts (#Microposts2014)*, pages 64–65.

Johannes Hoffart, Mohamed Amir Yosef, Ilaria Bordino, Hagen Fürstenau, Manfred Pinkal, Marc Spaniol, Bilyana Taneva, Stefan Thater, and Gerhard Weikum. 2011. Robust disambiguation of named entities in text. In *Proceedings of the Conference on Empirical Methods in Natural Language Processing*, EMNLP '11, pages 782–792, Stroudsburg, PA, USA. Association for Computational Linguistics.

Nicholas Kushmerick, Daniel S. Weld, and Robert Doorenbos. 1997. Wrapper induction for information extraction. In *Proc. IJCAI-97.*

Ndapandula Nakashole, Martin Theobald, and Gerhard Weikum. 2011. Scalable knowledge harvesting with high precision and high recall. In *Proceedings of the Fourth ACM International Conference on Web Search and Data Mining*, WSDM '11, pages 227–236, New York, NY, USA. ACM.

Fabian M. Suchanek, Gjergji Kasneci, and Gerhard Weikum. 2007. Yago: A core of semantic knowledge. In *Proceedings of the 16th International Conference on World Wide Web*, WWW '07, pages 697–706, New York, NY, USA. ACM.

Seed Selection for Distantly Supervised Web-Based Relation Extraction

Isabelle Augenstein
Department of Computer Science
The University of Sheffield
United Kingdom
i.augenstein@dcs.shef.ac.uk

Abstract

In this paper we consider the problem of distant supervision to extract relations (e.g. origin(musical artist, location)) for entities (e.g. 'The Beatles') of certain classes (e.g. musical artist) from Web pages by using background information from the Linking Open Data cloud to automatically label Web documents which are then used as training data for relation classifiers. Distant supervision approaches typically suffer from the problem of ambiguity when automatically labelling text, as well as the problem of incompleteness of background data to judge whether a mention is a true relation mention. This paper explores the hypothesis that simple statistical methods based on background data can help to filter unreliable training data and thus improve the precision of relation extractors. Experiments on a Web corpus show that an error reduction of 35% can be achieved by strategically selecting seed data.

1 Introduction

One important aspect to every relation extraction approach is how to annotate training and test data for learning classifiers. In the past, four different types of approaches for this have been proposed.
For *supervised* approaches, training and test data is annotated manually by one or several annotators. While this approach results in a high-quality corpus, it is very expensive and time-consuming. As a consequence, the corpora used tend to be small and biased towards a certain domain or type of text.
Unsupervised approaches do not need annotated data for training; they instead cluster similar word sequences and generalise them to relations. Although unsupervised aproaches can process very large amounts of data, resulting relations are hard to map to particular schemas. In addition, Fader et al. (2011) observe that these approaches often produce uninformative or incoherent extractions.
Semi-supervised methods are methods that only require a small number of seed instances. Hand-crafted seeds are used to extract patterns from a corpus, which are then used to extract more instances and those again to extract new patterns in an iterative way. However, since many iterations are needed, these methods are prone to semantic drift, i.e. an unwanted shift of meaning. As a consequence these methods require a certain amount of human effort - to create seeds initially and also to help keep systems 'on track'.
A fourth group of approaches, *distant supervision* or *self-supervised* approaches, exploit big knowledge bases such as Freebase (2008) to automatically label entities in text and use the annotated text to extract features and train a classifier (Wu and Weld, 2007; Mintz et al., 2009). Unlike supervised systems, they do not require manual effort to label data and can be applied to large corpora. Since they extract relations which are defined by schemas, these approaches also do not produce informative or incoherent relations.
Distant supervision approaches are based on the following assumption (Mintz et al., 2009):
"If two entities participate in a relation, any sentence that contains those two entities might express that relation." In practice, if the information that two entities participate in a relation is contained in the knowledge base, whenever they appear in the same sentence, that sentence is used as positive training data for that relation. This heuristic causes problems if different entities have the same surface form. Consider

Proceedings of Third Workshop on Semantic Web and Information Extraction, pages 17–24,
Dublin, Ireland, 24 August, 2014.

the following example:
"*Let It Be* is the twelfth album by *The Beatles* which contains their hit single '*Let It Be*'."
In that sentence, the first mention of *Let It Be* is an example of the *album* relation, whereas the second mention is an example of the *track* relation. If both mentions are used as positive training examples for both relations, this impairs the learning of weights of the relation classifiers. We therefore argue for the careful selection of training data for distant supervision by using measures to discard highly ambiguous training examples. One further aspect that can be problematic when automatically creating negative training data is incompleteness. What Riedel et al. (2010) point out, and our observations also confirm, is that about 20%, or even more, of all true relation mentions in a corpus are not contained in Freebase, although it is a very big knowledge base.

The main contributions of this paper are: to propose and evaluate several measures for detecting and discarding unreliable seeds; and to document a distant supervision system for fine-grained class-based relation extraction on noisy data from the Web.

2 Distantly Supervised Relation Extraction

Distant supervision is defined as the automatic labelling of a corpus with properties, P and entities, E from a knowledge base, KB to train a classifier to learn to predict relations. Following previous distant supervision approaches, we only consider binary relations of the form (s, p, o), consisting of a subject, a predicate and an object (Mintz et al., 2009). We use the established Semantic Web formalisation, rather than unary and binary first order predicates, to reflect our special and consistent treatment of subjects versus objects. Each subject and object entity $e \in E$ has a set of lexicalisations, $L_e \subset L$. Furthermore, we consider only those subjects which have a particular Freebase class C.

3 Seed Selection

Before using the automatically labelled corpus to train a classifier, we include a seed selection step, which consist of several measures to discard unreliable seeds.

Ambiguity Within An Entity

Unam: Our first approach is to discard lexicalisations of objects if they are ambiguous for the subject entity, i.e. if a subject is related to two different objects which have the same lexicalisation, and express two different relations. To illustrate this, let us consider the problem outlined in the introduction again: *Let It Be* can be both an *album* and a *track* of the subject entity *The Beatles*, therefore we would like to discard *Let It Be* as a seed for the class *Musical Artist*. We measure the degree to which a lexicalisation $l \in L_o$ of an object o is ambiguous by the number of senses the lexicalisation has. For a given subject s, if we discover a lexicalisation for a related entity, i.e. $(s, p, o) \in KB$ and $l \in L_o$, then, since it may be the case that $l \in L_r$ for some $R \ni r \neq o$, where also $(s, q, r) \in KB$ for some $q \in P$, we say in this case that l has a "sense" o and r, giving rise to ambiguity. We then define A_l^s, the ambiguity of a lexicalisation with respect to the subject as follows: $A_l^s = |\{e \mid l \in L_o \cap L_w \wedge (s, p, o) \in KB \wedge (s, v, w) \in KB \wedge w \neq o\}|$.

Ambiguity Across Classes

In addition to being ambiguous for a subject of a specific class, lexicalisations of objects can be ambiguous across classes. Our assumption is that the more senses an object lexicalisation has, the more likely it is that that object occurence is confused with an object lexicalisation of a different property of any class. An example for this are common names of book authors or common genres as in the sentence "*Jack* mentioned that he read *On the Road*", in which *Jack* is falsely recognised as the author Jack Kerouac.
Stop: One type of very ambiguous words with many senses are stop words. Since some objects of relations in our training set might have lexicalisations which are stop words, we discard those lexicalisations if they appear in a stop word list (we use the one described in Lewis et al. (2004)).
Stat: For other highly ambiguous lexicalisations of object entities our approach is to estimate cross-class ambiguity, i.e. to estimate how ambiguous a lexicalisation of an object is compared to other lexicalisations of objects of the same relation. If its ambiguity is comparatively low, we consider it a reliable seed,

otherwise we want to discard it. For the set of classes under consideration, we know the set of properties that apply, $D \subset P$ and can retrieve the set $\{o \mid (s, p, o) \in KB \wedge p \in D\}$, and retrieve the set of lexicalisations for each member, L_o. We then compute A_o, the number of senses for every lexicalisation of an object L_o, where $A_o = |\{o \mid \ \in L_o\}|$.
We view the number of senses of each lexicalisation of an object per relation as a frequency distribution. We then compute min, max, median ($Q2$), the lower ($Q1$) and the upper quartile ($Q3$) of those frequency distributions and compare it to the number of senses of each lexicalisation of an object. If $A_l > Q$, where Q is either $Q1$, $Q2$ or $Q3$ depending on the model, we discard the lexicalisation of the object.

Incompletess

One further aspect of knowledge bases that can be problematic when automatically creating negative training data is incompleteness. Our method for creating negative training data is to assume that all entities which appear in a sentence with the subject s, but are not in a relation with it according to the knowledge base, can be used as negative training data. Other distant supervision approaches (Mintz et al., 2009) follow a similar approach, but only use a random sample of unrelated entities pairs.
Incomp: Our approach is to discard negative training examples which are likely to be true relation mentions, but missing from the knowledge base. If we find a lexicalisation l where $\nexists o, p \ \cdot \ l \in L_o \wedge (s, p, o) \in KB$, then before we consider this a negative example we check if $\exists t \in C \cdot (t, q, r) \in KB$ and $l \in L_r$, i.e. if any of the properties of the class we examine has an object lexicalisation l.

4 System

4.1 Corpus

To create a corpus for Web relation extraction using Linked Data, three Freebase classes and their six to seven most prominent properties (see Table 1) are selected and their values retrieved using the Freebase API. To avoid noisy training data, entities which only have values for some of those relations were not used. This resulted in 1800 to 2200 entities per class which were split equally for training and test. For each entity, at most 10 Web pages were retrieved via the Google Search API using the search pattern ""*subject_entity*" *class property_name*", e.g. ""The Beatles" Musical Artist Origin" resulting in a total of 450,000 pages[1]. By adding the class, we expect the retrieved Web pages to be more relevant to our extraction task. For entities, Freebase distinguishes between the most prominant lexicalisation (the entity name) and other lexicalisations (entity aliases). We use the entity name for all of the search patterns.

Class	Property	Class	Property	Class	Property
Book	author	Musical Artist	album	Politician	birthdate
	characters		active (start)		birthplace
	publication date		active (end)		educational institution
	genre		genre		nationality
	ISBN		record label		party
	original language		origin		religion
			track		spouses

Table 1: Freebase classes and properties we use for our evaluation

4.2 NLP Pipeline

Text content is extracted from HTML pages using the jsoup API[2], which strips text from each element recurvisely. Each paragraph is then processed with Stanford CoreNLP[3] to split the text into sentences,

[1] URLs of those Web pages are available via `http://staffwww.dcs.shef.ac.uk/people/I.Augenstein/SWAIE2014/`
[2] `http://jsoup.org/`
[3] `http://nlp.stanford.edu/software/corenlp.shtml`

tokenise, POS tag it and normalise time expressions. Named entities are classified using the 7 class (time, location, organisation, person, money, percent, date) named entity model.

4.3 Relation candidate identification

Some of the objects of relations cannot be categorised according to the 7 named entity (NE) classes detected by the Stanford named entity classifier (NERC) and are therefore not recognised, for example *MusicalArtist:album* or *Book:genre*. Therefore, in addition to recognising entities with Stanford NERC, we also implement our own named entity recogniser (NER), which only recognises entity boundaries, but does not classify them. To detect entity boundaries, we recognise sequences of nouns and sequences of capitalised words and apply both greedy and non-greedy matching. For greedy matching, we consider whole noun phrases and for non-greedy matching all subsequences starting with the first word of the those phrases, i.e. for 'science fiction book', we would consider 'science fiction book', 'science fiction' and 'book' as candidates. The reason to do greedy as well as non-greedy matching is because the lexicalisation of an object does not always span a whole noun phrase, e.g. while 'science fiction' is a lexicalisation of an object of *Book:genre*, 'science fiction book' is not. However, for *MusicalArtist:genre*, 'pop music' would be a valid lexicalisation of an object. We also recognise short sequences of words in quotes. This is because lexicalisation of objects of *MusicalArtist:track* and *MusicalArtist:album* often appear in quotes, but are not necessarily noun phrases.

4.4 Identifying Relation Candidates and Selecting Seeds

The next step is to identify which sentences potentially express relations. We only use sentences from Web pages which were retrieved using a query which contains the subject of the relation. We then select, or rather discard seeds for training according to the different methods outlined in Section 3. Our *baseline* model does not discard any training seeds.

4.5 Features

Our system uses some of the features described in Mintz et al. (2009), and other standard lexical features and named entity features:

- The object occurrence
- The bag of words of the occurrence
- The number of words of the occurrence
- The named entity class of the occurrence assigned by the 7-class Stanford NERC
- A flag indicating if the object or the subject entity came first in the sentence
- The sequence of part of speech (POS) tags of the words between the subject and the occurrence
- The bag of words between the subject and the occurrence
- The pattern of words between the subject entity and the occurrence (all words except for nouns, verbs, adjectives and adverbs are replaced with their POS tag, nouns are replaced with their named entity class if a named entity class is available)
- Any nouns, verbs, adjectives, adverbs or NEs in a 3-word window to the left of the occurrence
- Any nouns, verbs, adjectives, adverbs or NEs in a 3-word window to the right of the occurrence

4.6 Classifier and Models

As a classifier, we choose a first-order conditional random field model (Lafferty et al., 2001). We use the software CRFSuite[4] and L-BFGS (Nocedal, 1980) for training our classifiers. We train one classifier per Freebase class and model. Our models only differ in the way training data is selected (see Section 3). The models are then used to classify each object candidate into one of the relations of the Freebase class or NONE (no relation).

---

[4]http://www.chokkan.org/software/crfsuite/

4.7 Merging and Ranking Results

We understand relation extraction as the task of predicting the relations which can be found in a corpus. While some approaches aim at correctly predicting every single mention of a relation seperately, we instead choose to aggregate predictions of relation mentions. For every Freebase class, we get all relation mentions from the corpus and the classifier's confidence values for Freebase classes assigned to object occurences. There are usually several different predictions, e.g. the same occurence could be predicted to be *MusicalArtist:album*, *MusicalArtist:origin* and *MusicalArtist:NONE*. By aggregating relation mentions across documents we have increased chances of choosing the right relation, since some contexts of occurences are inconclusive or ambiguous and thus the classifier chooses the wrong property wfor those. For a given lexicalisation l, representing an object to which the subject is related, the classifier gives each object occurence a prediction which is the combination of a predicted relation and a confidence. We collect these across the chosen documents to form a set of confidence values, for each predicted relation, per lexicalisation E_p^l. For instance if the lexicalisation l occurs three times across the documents and is predicted to represent an object to relation p_1 once with confidence 0.2, and in other cases to represent the object to relation p_2 with confidence 0.1 and 0.5 respectively, then $E_{p_1}^l = 0.2$ and $E_{p_2}^l = \{0.1, 0.5\}$. In order to form an aggregated confidence for each relation with respect to the lexicalisation, g_l^p, we calculate the mean average for each such set and normalise across relations, as follows: $g_p^l = \overline{E_p^l} \cdot \frac{|E_p^l|}{\sum_{q \in P} |E_q^l|}$

5 Evaluation

5.1 Corpus

Although we automatically annotate the training and test part of the Web corpus with properties, we hand-annotate a portion of the test corpus. The portion of the corpus we manually annotate is the one which has *NONE* predictions for object occurrences, i.e. for which occurences do not have a representation in Freebase. They could either get *NONE* predictions because they are not relation mentions, or because they are missing from Freebase. We find that on average 45% of the occurences which are predicted by our models are true relation mentions, but missing from Freebase. Note that some of the automatically evaluated positive predictions could in fact be false positives.

5.2 Results

Figures 1 and 2 show the precision with respect to confidence and precision@K for our self-supervised relation extraction models which only differ in the way training data is selected, as described in Section 3.

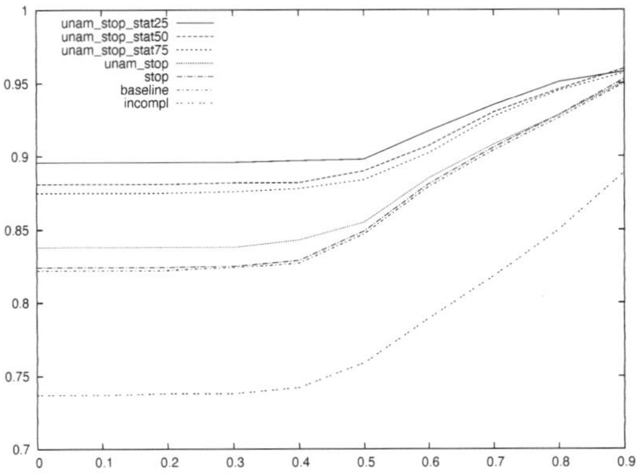

Figure 1: Precision / confidence graph

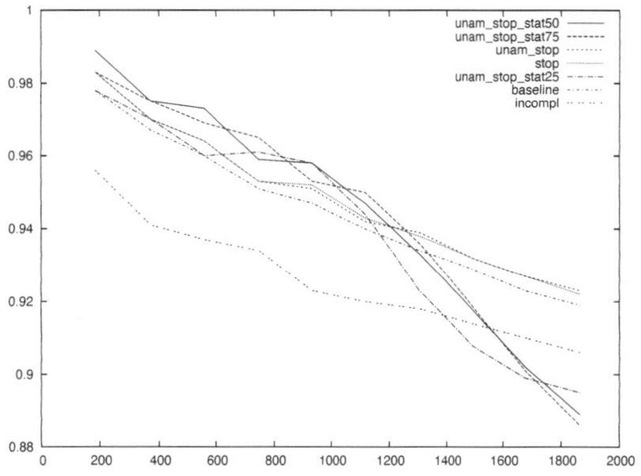

Figure 2: Precision@K

Figure 1 shows the precision of our models on the y-axis with respect to a cutoff at a minimum confidence displayed on the x-axis. The precision at a minimum confidence of 0 is equivalent to the precision over the whole test corpus. For all of the models, the precision rises with increasing confidence, which means our confidence measure succeeds at ranking results by precision. With respect to the baseline which does not filter seeds, our best-performing model increases the total precision from 0.825 to 0.896, which is a total error reduction of 35%. We achieve the best results in terms of total precision with the model unam_stop_stat25, which filters lexicalisations which are ambiguous for a subject, filters lexicalisations which are stop words and filters lexicalisations with an ambiguity value higher than the lower quartile of the distribution for the relation in question. The worst-performing model is, surprisingly, *incompl*, the model we built to discard negative training data which are likely to be true relation mentions, but missing from the knowledge base. We discuss this further in Section 8. Figures 2 shows the precision, sorted by confidence, for the K highest ranked documents. We decided to use the precision@K measure instead of computing recall because it is not feasible to manually annotate 450,000 Web pages with relation mentions. Note, however, that distant supervision is not aimed at high recall anyway - because only sentences which contain both the subject and the object entity explicitely are used, many relation mentions will be missed out on. The highest value on the x-axis is the number of predicted relations of the model with the smallest number of predicted relations. The models which filter seeds improve all above the baseline in terms of precision@K for 0% to about 65% of the maximum K, from 65% to 100%, only stop and unam_stop improve on the baseline.

6 Discussion

Although we cannot directly compare our results to that of other distantly supervised relation extraction models because we use different evaluation data and a different set of relations, our baseline model, which has a total precision of 0.825, as well as our best-performing model, which has a total precision of 0.896 seem to be perform as well as, if not better than previous systems. Overall, our seed selection methods seem to perform well at removing unreliable training data to improve precision.

What is still unsuccessful is our *incompl* model. The idea behind it was that relations which, for a given subject, have more than one object (e.g. *Book:genre*) are prone to be "incomplete" - the objects in the knowledge base are often just the most prominent ones and other objects, which could be discovered from text, are missing. When annotating training data for distant supervision, those missing objects would be considered negative training data, which could potentially be harmful for training. However, just assuming that all negative training examples could potentially be false negatives if they match one of the objects does not lead to improved results. One of the reasons for this could be that most of those potential false negatives are instead objects of relations which expect the same kinds of values - and thus crucial for training the models. Some relations for which we observed this are are *Book:originalLanguage* and *Book:translations*, as well as *Book:firstPublicationDate* and *Book:dateWritten*. Interestingly, neither *Book:originalLanguage* nor *Book:firstPublicationDate* are n:n relations.

7 Related Work

While lots of approaches in the past have focused on supervised, unsupervised (Yates et al., 2007; Fader et al., 2011) or semi-supervised relation extraction (Hearst, 1992; Carlson et al., 2010), there have also been some distantly supervised relation extraction approaches in the past few years, which aim at exploiting background knowledge for relation extraction, most of them for extracting relations from Wikipedia.

Mintz et al. (2009) describe one of the first distant supervision approaches which aims at extracting relations between entities in Wikipedia for the most frequent relations in Freebase. They report precision of about 0.68 for their highest ranked 10% of results depending what features they used. In contrast to our approach, Mintz et al. do not experiment with changing the distance supervision assumption or removing ambiguous training data, they also do not use fine-grained relations and their approach is not class-based. Nguyen et al. (2011)'s approach is very similar to that of Mintz et al. (2009), except that they use a different knowledge base, YAGO (Suchanek et al., 2008). They use a Wikipedia-based NERC, which, like the Stanford NERC classifies entities into persons, relations and organisations. They report a precision of 0.914 for their whole test set, however, those results might be skewed by the fact that YAGO is a knowledge based derived from Wikipedia.

A few strategies for seed selection for distant supervision have already been investigated: At-least-one models (Hoffmann et al., 2011; Surdeanu et al., 2012; Riedel et al., 2010; Yao et al., 2010; Min et al., 2013), hierarchical topic models (Alfonseca et al., 2012; Roth and Klakow, 2013), pattern correlations (Takamatsu et al., 2012), and an information retrieval approach (Xu et al., 2013). At-least-one models (Hoffmann et al., 2011; Surdeanu et al., 2012; Riedel et al., 2010; Yao et al., 2010; Min et al., 2013) are based on the idea that "if two entities particpate in a relation, at least one sentence that mentions these two entities might express that relation". While positive results have been reported for those models, Riedel et al. (Riedel et al., 2010) argues that it is challenging to train those models because they are quite complex. Hierarchical topic models (Alfonseca et al., 2012; Roth and Klakow, 2013) assume that the context of a relation is either specific for the pair of entities, the relation, or neither. Min et al. (Min et al., 2013) further propose a 4-layer hierarchical model to only learn from positive examples to address the problem of incomplete negative training data. Pattern correlations (Takamatsu et al., 2012) are also based on the idea of examining the context of pairs of entities, but instead of using a topic model as a pre-processing step for learning extraction patterns, they first learn patterns and then use a probabilistic graphical model to group extraction patterns. Xu et al. (Xu et al., 2013) propose a two-step model based on the idea of pseudo-relevance feedback which first ranks extractions, then only uses the highest ranked ones to re-train their model. Our research is based on a different assumption: Instead of trying to address the problem of noisy training data by using more complicated multi-stage machine learning models, we want to examine how background data can be even further exploited by testing if simple statistical methods based on data already present in the knowledge base can help to filter unreliable training data.

8 Future Work

In this paper, we have documented and evaluated an approach to discard unreliable seed data for distantly supervised relation extraction. Our two hypotheses were that discarding highly ambiguous relation mentions and discarding unreliable negative training seeds could help to improve precision of self-supervised relation extraction models. While our evaluation indicates that discarding highly ambiguous relation mentions based on simple statistical methods helps to improve the precision of distantly supervised relation extraction systems, discarding negative training data does not. We have also described our distantly supervised relation extraction system, which, unlike other previous systems learns to extract from Web pages and also learns to extract fine-grained relations for specific classes instead of relations which are applicable to several broad classes.

In future work, we want to work on increasing the number of extractions for distant supervision systems: The distant supervision assumption requires sentences to contain both the subject and the object of a relation. While this ensures high precision and is acceptable for creating training data, most sentences - at least those in Web documents - do not mention the subject of relations explicitly and we thus miss out on a lot of data to extract from. We further want to extend our distant supervision approach to extract information not only from free text, but also from lists and relational tables from Web pages. Finally, we would like to train distantly supervised models for entity classification to assist relation extraction. A more detailed description of future work can also be found in Augenstein (2014).

Acknowledgements

We thank Barry Norton, Diana Maynard, as well as the anonymous reviewers for their valuable feedback. This research was partly supported by the EPSRC funded project LODIE: Linked Open Data for Information Extraction, EP/J019488/1.

References

Enrique Alfonseca, Katja Filippova, Jean-Yves Delort, and Guillermo Garrido. 2012. Pattern Learning for Relation Extraction with a Hierarchical Topic Model. In *Proceedings of the 50th Annual Meeting of the Association for Computational Linguistics: Short Papers*, volume 2, pages 54–59.

Isabelle Augenstein. 2014. Joint Information Extraction from the Web using Linked Data. *Doctoral Consortium Proceedings of the 13th International Semantic Web Conference*. to appear.

Kurt Bollacker, Colin Evans, Praveen Paritosh, Tim Sturge, and Jamie Taylor. 2008. Freebase: A Collaboratively Created Graph Database For Structuring Human Knowledge. In *Proceedings of the 2008 ACM SIGMOD international conference on Management of data*, pages 1247–1250.

A. Carlson, J. Betteridge, B. Kisiel, B. Settles, E.R. Hruschka Jr., and T.M. Mitchell. 2010. Toward an Architecture for Never-Ending Language Learning. In *Proceedings of the Conference on Artificial Intelligence*, pages 1306–1313.

Anthony Fader, Stephen Soderland, and Oren Etzioni. 2011. Identifying relations for open information extraction. In *Proceedings of the Conference on Empirical Methods in Natural Language Processing*, pages 1535–1545.

Marti A. Hearst. 1992. Automatic Acquisition of Hyponyms from Large Text Corpora. In *Proceedings of the 14th International Conference on Computational Linguistics*, pages 539–545.

Raphael Hoffmann, Congle Zhang, Xiao Ling, Luke S. Zettlemoyer, and Daniel S. Weld. 2011. Knowledge-Based Weak Supervision for Information Extraction of Overlapping Relations. In *Proceedings of the 49th Annual Meeting of the Association for Computational Linguistics*, pages 541–550.

John Lafferty, Andrew McCallum, and Fernando Pereira. 2001. Conditional random fields: Probabilistic models for segmenting and labeling sequence data. In *Proceedings of the 18th International Conference on Machine Learning*, pages 282–289.

D. D. Lewis, Y. Yang, T. G. Rose, and F. Li. 2004. RCV1: A New Benchmark Collection for Text Categorization Research. *Journal of Machine Learning Research*, 5:361–397.

Bonan Min, Ralph Grishman, Li Wan, Chang Wang, and David Gondek. 2013. Distant Supervision for Relation Extraction with an Incomplete Knowledge Base. In *Proceedings of HLT-NAACL*, pages 777–782.

Mike Mintz, Steven Bills, Rion Snow, and Dan Jurafsky. 2009. Distant supervision for relation extraction without labeled data. In *Proceedings of ACL-IJCNLP*, volume 2, pages 1003–1011.

Truc-Vien T. Nguyen and Alessandro Moschitti. 2011. End-to-End Relation Extraction Using Distant Supervision from External Semantic Repositories. In *Proceedings of the 50th Annual Meeting of the Association for Computational Linguistics: Short Papers*, volume 2, pages 277–282.

Jorge Nocedal. 1980. Updating Quasi-Newton Matrices with Limited Storage. *Mathematics of Computation*, 35(151):773–782.

Sebastian Riedel, Limin Yao, and Andrew McCallum. 2010. Modeling Relations and Their Mentions without Labeled Text. In *Proceedings of the 2010 European conference on Machine learning and knowledge discovery in databases: Part III*, pages 148–163.

Benjamin Roth and Dietrich Klakow. 2013. Combining Generative and Discriminative Model Scores for Distant Supervision. In *Proceedings of the 2013 Conference on Empirical Methods in Natural Language Processing*, pages 24–29.

Fabian M Suchanek, Gjergji Kasneci, and Gerhard Weikum. 2008. YAGO: A Large Ontology from Wikipedia and WordNet. *Web Semantics: Science, Services and Agents on the World Wide Web*, 6(3):203–217.

Mihai Surdeanu, Julie Tibshirani, Ramesh Nallapati, and Christopher D. Manning. 2012. Multi-instance Multi-label Learning for Relation Extraction. In *Proceedings of EMNLP-CoNLL*, pages 455–465.

Shingo Takamatsu, Issei Sato, and Hiroshi Nakagawa. 2012. Reducing Wrong Labels in Distant Supervision for Relation Extraction. In *Proceedings of the 50th Annual Meeting of the Association for Computational Linguistics*, pages 721–729.

Fei Wu and Daniel S. Weld. 2007. Autonomously Semantifying Wikipedia. In *Proceedings of the Sixteenth ACM Conference on Information and Knowledge Management*, pages 41–50.

Wei Xu, Raphael Hoffmann, Le Zhao, and Ralph Grishman. 2013. Filling Knowledge Base Gaps for Distant Supervision of Relation Extraction. In *Proceedings of the 51st Annual Meeting of the Association for Computational Linguistics*, pages 665–670.

Limin Yao, Sebastian Riedel, and Andrew McCallum. 2010. Collective Cross-document Relation Extraction Without Labelled Data. In *Proceedings of the 2010 Conference on Empirical Methods in Natural Language Processing*, pages 1013–1023.

Alexander Yates, Michael Cafarella, Michele Banko, Oren Etzioni, Matthew Broadhead, and Stephen Soderland. 2007. TextRunner: Open Information Extraction on the Web. In *Proceedings of HLT-NAACL: Demonstrations*, pages 25–26.

Ontology-based Extraction of Structured Information from Publications on Preclinical Experiments for Spinal Cord Injury Treatments

Benjamin Paassen*, Andreas Stöckel*, Raphael Dickfelder*, Jan Philip Göpfert*, Tarek Kirchhoffer§, Nicole Brazda‡,§, Hans Werner Müller‡,§, Roman Klinger*, Matthias Hartung*, Philipp Cimiano*[1]

*Semantic Computing Group, CIT-EC, Bielefeld University, 33615 Bielefeld, Germany
‡Molecular Neurobiology, Neurology, HHU Düsseldorf, 40225 Düsseldorf, Germany
§Center for Neuronal Regeneration, Life Science Center, 40225 Düsseldorf, Germany

{bpaassen,astoecke,rdickfel,jgoepfert}@techfak.uni-bielefeld.de
tarek.kirchhoffer@cnr.de, {nicole.brazda,hanswerner.mueller}@uni-duesseldorf.de
{rklinger,mhartung,cimiano}@cit-ec.uni-bielefeld.de

Abstract

Preclinical research in the field of central nervous system trauma advances at a fast pace, currently yielding over 8,000 new publications per year, at an exponentially growing rate. This amount of published information by far exceeds the capacity of individual scientists to read and understand the relevant literature. So far, no clinical trial has led to therapeutic approaches which achieve functional recovery in human patients.

In this paper, we describe a first prototype of an ontology-based information extraction system that automatically extracts relevant preclinical knowledge about spinal cord injury treatments from natural language text by recognizing participating entity classes and linking them to each other. The evaluation on an independent test corpus of manually annotated full text articles shows a macro-average F_1 measure of 0.74 with precision 0.68 and recall 0.81 on the task of identifying entities participating in relations.

1 Introduction

Injury to the central nervous system of adult mammals typically results in lasting deficits, like permanent motor and sensor impairments, due to a lack of profound neural regeneration. Specifically, patients who have sustained spinal cord injuries (SCI) usually remain partially paralyzed for the rest of their lives. Preclinical research in the field of central nervous system trauma advances at fast pace, currently yielding over 8,000 new publications per year, at an exponentially growing rate, with a total amount of approximately 160,000 PubMed-listed papers today.[2]

However, translational neuroscience faces a strong disproportion between the immense preclinical research effort and the lack of successful clinical trials in SCI therapy: So far, no therapeutic approach has led to functional recovery in human patients (Filli and Schwab, 2012). As the vast amount of published information by far exceeds the capacity of individual scientists to read and understand the relevant knowledge (Lok, 2010), the selection of promising therapeutic interventions for clinical trials is notoriously based on incomplete information (Prinz et al., 2011; Steward et al., 2012).

Thus, automatic information extraction methods are needed to gather structured, actionable knowledge from large amounts of unstructured text that describe outcomes of preclinical experiments in the SCI domain. Being stored in a database, such knowledge provides a highly valuable resource enabling curators and researchers to objectively assess the prospective success of experimental therapies in humans, and supports the cost-effective execution of meta studies based on all previously published data. First steps towards such a database have already been undertaken by manually extracting the desired information from a limited number of papers (Brazda et al., 2013), which is not feasible on a large scale, though.

In this paper, we present a first prototype of an automated ontology-based information extraction system for the acquisition of structured knowledge about experimental SCI therapies. As main contributions, we point out the highly relational problem structure by describing the entity classes and relations relevant for

[1] The first four authors contributed equally.
[2] As in this query to the database PubMed (link to http://www.ncbi.nlm.nih.gov/pubmed), as of April 2014.

Proceedings of Third Workshop on Semantic Web and Information Extraction, pages 25–32,
Dublin, Ireland, 24 August, 2014.

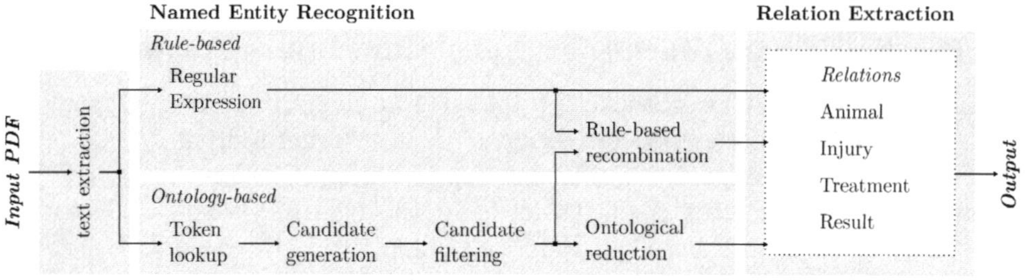

Figure 1: Workflow of our implementation, from the input PDF document to the generation of the output relations. Named entity recognition is described in Section 3.1, relation extraction in Section 3.2.

knowledge representation in the domain, and provide a cascaded workflow that is capable of extracting these relational structures from unstructured text with an average F_1 measure of 0.74.

2 Related Work

Our workflow for acquiring structured information in the domain of spinal cord injury treatments is an example of ontology-based information extraction systems (Wimalasuriya and Dou, 2010): Large amounts of unstructured natural language text are processed through a mechanism guided by an ontology, in order to extract predefined types of information. Our long-term goal is to represent all relevant information on SCI treatments in structured form, similar to other automatically populated databases in the biomedical domain, such as STRING-DB for protein-protein interactions (Franceschini et al., 2013), among others.

A strong focus in biomedical information extraction has long been on named entity recognition, for which machine-learning solutions such as conditional random fields (Lafferty et al., 2001) or dictionary-based systems (Schuemie et al., 2007; Hanisch et al., 2005; Hakenberg et al., 2011) are available which tackle the respective problem with decent performance and for specific entity classes such as organisms (Pafilis et al., 2013) or symptoms (Savova et al., 2010; Jimeno et al., 2008). A detailed overview on named entity recognition, covering other domains as well, can be found in Nadeau and Sekine (2007).

The use case described in this paper, however, involves a highly relational problem structure in the sense that individual facts or relations have to be aggregated in order to yield accurate, holistic domain knowledge, which corresponds most closely to the problem structure encountered in event extraction, as triggered by the ACE program (Doddington et al., 2004; Ji and Grishman, 2008; Strassel et al., 2008), and the BioNLP shared task series (Nedellec et al., 2013; Tsujii et al., 2011; Tsujii, 2009). General semantic search engines in the biomedical domain mainly focus on isolated entities. Relations are typically only taken into account by co-occurrence on abstract or sentence level. Examples for such search engines include GoPubMed (Doms and Schroeder, 2005), SCAIView (Hofmann Apitius et al., 2008), and GeneView (Thomas et al., 2012).

With respect to the extraction methodology, our work is similar to Saggion et al. (2007) and Buitelaar et al. (2008), in that a combination of gazetteers and extraction rules is derived from the underlying ontology, in order to adapt the workflow to the domain of interest. A schema in terms of a reporting standard has recently been proposed by the MIASCI-consortium (Lemmon et al., 2014, Minimum Information About a Spinal Cord Injury Experiment). To the best of our knowledge, our work is the first attempt at automated information extraction in the SCI domain.

3 Method and Architecture

An illustration of the proposed workflow is shown in Figure 1. Based on the unstructured information management architecture (UIMA, Ferrucci and Lally (2004)), full text PDF documents serve as input to the workflow. Plain text and structural information are extracted from these documents using Apache PDFBox[3].

The proposed system extracts *relations* which we define as templates that contain slots, each of which is to be filled by an instance of a particular entity class (*cf.* Table 1). At the same time, a particular instance can be a filler for different slots (*cf.* Figure 2). We argue that a relational approach is essential to information extraction in the SCI domain as (i) many instances of entity classes found in the text do not convey relevant

[3]Apache PDFBox – A Java PDF Library `http://pdfbox.apache.org/`

Relation	Entity Class	Example	Method	Resource	Count
	Integer	"42", "2k", "1,000"	R	Regular Expressions	
	Float	"4.23", "$8.12 \cdot 10^{-8}$"	R	Regular Expressions	
	Roman Number	"XII", "MCLXII"	R	Regular Expressions	
	Word Number	"seventy-six"	O	*Word Number List*	99
	Range	"2-4"	R	QTY + PARTICLE + QTY	
	Language Quantifier	"many", "all"	O	*Quantifier List*	11
	Time	"2 h", "14 weeks"	R	QTY + TIME UNIT	
	Duration	"for 2h"	R	PARTICLE + TIME	
	Organism	"dog", "rat", "mice"	O	NCBI Taxonomy	67657
	Laboratory Animal	"Long-Evans rats"	O	*Special Laboratory Animals*	5
	Sex	"male", "female"	O	*Gender List*	2
Animal	Exact Age	"14 weeks old"	R	TIME + AGE PARTICLE	
	Age	"adult", "juvenile"	O	*Age Expressions*	2
	Weight	"200 g"	R	QTY + WEIGHT UNIT	
	Number	"44", "seventy-six"	R	QTY	
	Injury Type	"compression"	O	*Injury Type List*	7
Injury	Injury Device	"NYU Impactor"	O	*Injury Device List*	21
	Vertebral Position	"T4", "T8-9"	R	Regular Expressions	
	Injury Height	"cervical", "thoracic"	O	*Injury Height Expressions*	4
	Drug	"EPO", "inosine"	O	MeSH	14000
Treatment	Delivery	"subcutaneous", "i.v."	O	*Delivery Dictionary*	34
	Dosage	"14 ml/kg"	R	QTY + UNIT	
	Investigation Method	"walking analysis"	O	*Method List*	117
Result	Significance	"significant"	O	*Significance Quantifiers*	2
	Trend	"decreased", "improved"	O	*Trend Dictionary*	4
	p Value	"$p < 0.05$"	R	P + QTY	4

Table 1: A detailed list of relations and the entity classes whose instances are valid slot fillers for them. Examples for instances of each entity class are also shown, as well as the extraction method, and resources used for extraction. Instances are either extracted from the text using regular expressions (R) or on a lookup in our ontology database (O). Resources in *italics* were specifically created for this application, resources in SMALL CAPITALS are regular expression-based recombinations of other entities. Entity classes in bold face are *required* arguments for relation extraction (*cf.* Section 3.2). The count specifies the number of elements in the respective resource.

information on their own, but only in combination with other instances (*e. g.*, surgical devices mentioned in the text are only relevant if used to inflict a spincal cord injury to the animals in an experimental group), and (ii) a holistic picture of a preclinical experiment can only be captured by aggregating several relations (*e. g.*, a certain p value being mentioned in the text implies a particular treatment of one group of animals to be significantly different from another treatment of a control group).

We take four relations (*Animal*, *Injury*, *Treatment* and *Result*) into account which capture the semantic essence of a preclinical experiment: Laboratory animals are injured, then treated and the effect of the treatment is measured. Table 1 provides an overview of all entity classes and relations. The workflow consists of two steps: Firstly, rule- and ontology-based named entity recognition (NER) is performed (*cf.* Section 3.1). Secondly, the pool of entities recognized during NER serves as a basis for relation extraction (*cf.* Section 3.2).

3.1 Ontology-based Named Entity Recognition

We store ontological information in a relational database as a set of directed graphs, accompanied by a dictionary for efficient token lookup. Each entity is stored with possible linguistic surface forms (*e. g.*, "Wistar rats" as a surface form of the *Wistar rat* entity from the class *Laboratory Animal*). Each surface form s is tokenized (on white space and non-alphanumeric symbols, including transformation to lowercase, *e. g.*, leading to tokens "wistar" and "rats") and normalized (stemming, removal of special characters and stop words) resulting in a set of *dictionary keys* (*e. g.*, "wistar" and "rat"). The resources used as content for the ontology are shown in Table 1. We use specifically crafted resources for our use case[4] as well as the

[4]Resources built specifically are made publicly available at `http://opensource.cit-ec.de/projects/scic`

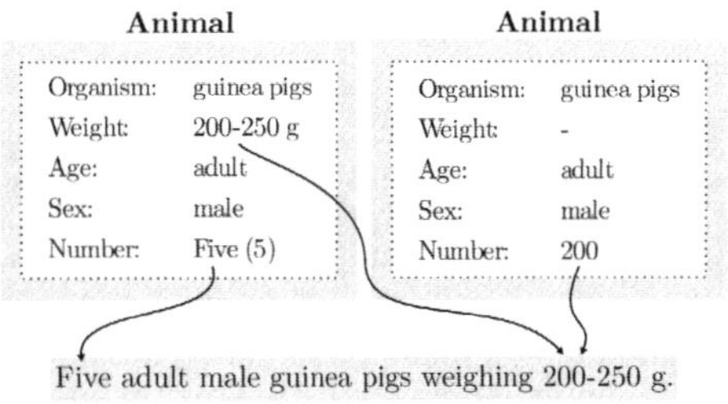

Figure 2: Two example instances of the *Animal* relation that can be generated from the same text. Given its entity class, the number 200 is a valid filler for the 'number' slot as well as the 'weight' slot. Both candidates are generated and ranked according to their probability (*cf.* Equation 4). The manually defined constraints of p_{sem} ensure that 200 cannot fill both slots at the same time.

NCBI taxonomy[5] and the Medical Subject Headings[6] (MeSH). The process of ontology-based NER consists of (i) *token lookup* in the dictionary, (ii) *candidate generation*, (iii) *probabilistic candidate filtering* and (iv) *ontological reduction* (*cf.* Figure 1).

Token lookup. For each token t in the document, the corresponding surface form tokens $\mathbf{s}_t$ are retrieved from the database. A *confidence value* p_{conf} based on the Damerau-Levenshtein-Distance without swaps (dld, Damerau (1964)) is calculated as

$$p_{\text{conf}}(t, \mathbf{s}_t) := \max\left\{0, 1 - \min_{t' \in \mathbf{s}_t} \frac{\text{dld}(t', t)}{|t'|}\right\}, \tag{1}$$

where $|t|$ denotes the number of characters in token t. Assuming to find t = "rat" in the text with the according surface form $\mathbf{s}_t$ = ("wistar", "rats"), $p_{\text{conf}}(t, \mathbf{s}_t) = 1 - \frac{1}{4} = 0.75$. Tokens with $p_{\text{conf}} < 0.5$ are discarded.

Candidate generation. A candidate $\mathbf{h}$ for matching the surface form tokens $\mathbf{s}_\mathbf{h}$ is a list of tokens $(t_1^\mathbf{h}, \dots, t_n^\mathbf{h})$ from the text. Candidates are constructed using all possible combinations of matching tokens for each surface form token (as retrieved above). To keep this tractable, we restrict the search space to combinations with the proximity $d(t_k^h, t_\ell^h) \leq 9$ for all $t_k^h, t_\ell^h \in \mathbf{h}$, where $d(u, v) := N_W(u, v) + 3 \cdot N_S(u, v) + 10 \cdot N_P(u, v)$ models the distance between two tokens u and v in the text with N_W, N_S, N_P denoting the number of words, sentences and paragraphs between u and v. In our example, a candidate would be $\mathbf{h}$ = ("rat").

Candidate filtering. For a candidate $\mathbf{h}$ and the surface form tokens $\mathbf{s}_\mathbf{h}$ it refers to, we calculate a total *match probability*, taking into account the distance $d(u, v)$ of all tokens in the candidate, the confidence $p_{\text{conf}}(t', \mathbf{s}_\mathbf{h})$ that the token actually belongs to the surface form, and the ratio $\sum_{t' \in \mathbf{h}} |t'| / \sum_{t \in \mathbf{s}_\mathbf{h}} |t|$ of the surface form tokens covered by the candidate:

$$p_{\text{match}}(\mathbf{h}, \mathbf{s}_\mathbf{h}) = \frac{1}{\sum_{t \in \mathbf{s}_\mathbf{h}} |t|} \max_{t \in \mathbf{h}} \sum_{t' \in \mathbf{h}} \left(p_{\text{dist}}^3(t, t') \cdot p_{\text{conf}}(t', \mathbf{s}_\mathbf{h}) \cdot |t'|\right), \tag{2}$$

$$\text{where } p_{\text{dist}}^\sigma(u, v) := \exp\left(-\frac{d(u, v)^2}{2\sigma^2}\right) \tag{3}$$

models the confidence that two tokens u and v belong together given their distance in the text. In our example of the candidate $\mathbf{h}$ = ("rat") with the surface form tokens $\mathbf{s}_\mathbf{h}$ = ("wistar", "rats") is $p_{\text{match}}(\mathbf{h}, \mathbf{s}_\mathbf{h}) = 1 \cdot 0.75 \cdot \frac{3}{6+4} = 0.225$. Candidates with $p_{\text{match}} < 0.7$ are discarded. The resulting set of all recognized candidates is denoted with H.

Ontological reduction. As the algorithm ignores the hierarchical information provided by the ontologies, we may obtain overlapping matches for ontologically related entities. Therefore, in case of overlapping entities that are related in an "is a" relationship in the ontology, only the more specific one is kept. Assume for instance the candidates "Rattus norvegicus" and "Rattus norvegicus albus", where the latter is more specific and therefore accepted.

3.2 Relation Extraction

We frame *relation extraction* as a template filling task such that each slot provided by a relation has to be assigned a filler of the correct entity class. Entity classes for the four relations of interest are shown in

[5]Sayers et al. (2012), database limited to vertebrates: `http://www.ncbi.nlm.nih.gov/taxonomy/?term=txid7742[ORGN`

[6]Lipscomb (2000), excerpt of drugs from Descriptor and Supplemental: `https://www.nlm.nih.gov/mesh/`

Table 1, where *required* slots are in bold face, whereas all other slots are *optional*.

The slot filling process is based on testing all combinations of appropriate entities taking into account their proximity and additional constraints. In more detail, we define the set of all recognized relations $\mathcal{R}_\theta$ of a type θ as

$$\mathcal{R}_\theta = \left\{ r^\theta \in \mathcal{P}(H) \;\middle|\; \frac{p_{\text{sem}}(r^\theta)}{n^\theta} \cdot \sum_{\mathbf{h} \in r^\theta, \mathbf{h} \neq g(r^\theta)} p_{\text{match}}(\mathbf{h}, \mathbf{s}^{\mathbf{h}}) \min_{t \in \mathbf{h}, t' \in g(r^\theta)} p_{\text{dist}}^{\sigma_\theta}(t, t') > 0.2 \right\} \quad (4)$$

where $\mathcal{P}(H)$ denotes the power set over all candidates H recognized by NER. $g(r^\theta)$ returns the filler for the *required* slot of r^θ, p_{match} and p_{dist} are defined as in Section 3.1 and p_{sem} implements manually defined constraints on r^θ: A wrongly typed filler h for one slot of r^θ leads to $p_{\text{sem}}(r^\theta) = 0$, as does a negative number in the *Number* slot of the *Animal* relation. Animal Numbers larger than 100 or Animal Weights smaller than 1 g or larger than 1 t are punished. All other cases lead to $p_{\text{sem}}(r^\theta) = 1$. Note that $p_{\text{match}}(\mathbf{h}, \mathbf{s}^{\mathbf{h}}) = 1$ for candidates h retrieved by rule-based entity recognition. Further, we set $\sigma_{\text{Animal}} = \sigma_{\text{Treatment}} = 6$, $\sigma_{\text{Injury}} = 10$ and $\sigma_{\text{Result}} = 15$.

4 Experiments

4.1 Data Set

The workflow is evaluated against an independent, manually annotated corpus of 32 complete papers which contain 1186 separate annotations of entities, produced by domain experts[7]. Information about relations is not provided in the corpus. Only entities which participate in the description of the preclinical experiment are marked. The frequencies of annotations among the different classes are shown in Table 2.

Overall	1186
Organism	58
Weight	32
Sex	33
Age	17
Injury Height	35
Injury Type	62
Injury Device	23
Drug	134
Dosage	106
Delivery	70
Investigation Method	129
Trend	219
Significance	137
p Value	131

Table 2: The number of annotations in our evaluation set for each entity class.

4.2 Experimental Settings

We evaluate the system with regard to two different tasks: *extraction* ("Is the approach able to extract relevant information from the text, without regard to the exact location of the information?") and *annotation* ("Is the system able to annotate relevant information at the correct location as indicated by medical experts?"). Furthermore, we distinguish between an *all instances* setting, where we consider all instances independently, and a *fillers only* setting, where only those annotations in the system output are considered, that are fillers in a relation (*i.e.* the fillers only-setting evaluates a subset of the all instances-setting). The relation extraction procedure is not evaluated separately. For each setting, we report precision, recall, and F_1 measure.

Taking the architecture into account, we have the following hypotheses: (i) For the *all instances* setting we expect high recall, but low precision. (ii) For the *fillers only* setting, precision should increase notably. (iii) Comparing the *all entities* and the *fillers only* setting, recall should remain at the same level. We therefore expect the *extraction* task to be simpler than the *annotation* task: For any information to be annotated at the correct position, it must have been extracted correctly. On the other hand, information that has been extracted correctly, can still be found at a 'wrong' location in the text. Thus, we expect a drop of precision and recall when moving from *extraction* to *annotation*.

4.3 Results

The results are presented in Table 3: For each relation mentioned in Section 3, and the entity classes participating in it, we report precision, recall and F_1-measure[8]. This is done for all four combinations of setting and task. For each relation we also provide the macro-average of precision, recall and F_1-measure over all entity classes considered in that relation and the overall average.

[7]Performed in Protégé `http://protege.stanford.edu/` with the plug-in Knowtator `http://knowtator.sourceforge.net/` (Ogren, 2006)

[8]Note that *VertebralPosition* and *InjuryHeight* are merged in the result table, as are *Organism* and *Laboratory Animal* and *Age* and *Exact Age*. The *Animal Number* was excluded from the evaluation as it has not been annotated in our evaluation set.

Task	Extraction						Annotation					
Setting	All Instances			Fillers Only			All Instances			Fillers Only		
Entity Class	Prec.	Rec.	F_1	Prec.	Rec.	F_1	Prec.	Rec.	F_1	Prec.	Rec.	F_1
Overall Average	0.58	0.95	0.72	0.68	0.81	0.74	0.13	0.77	0.22	0.21	0.51	0.30
***Animal* Average**	0.62	0.99	0.76	0.82	0.94	0.87	0.12	0.91	0.21	0.31	0.81	0.44
Organism	0.41	1.00	0.58	0.88	0.90	0.89	0.02	1.00	0.04	0.24	0.66	0.35
Weight	0.20	1.00	0.33	0.52	0.94	0.67	0.08	0.97	0.15	0.49	0.91	0.64
Sex	0.85	0.99	0.91	0.87	0.98	0.92	0.18	0.94	0.30	0.26	0.94	0.41
Age	1.00	0.95	0.97	1.00	0.93	0.96	0.19	0.71	0.30	0.23	0.71	0.35
***Injury* Average**	0.63	0.94	0.76	0.74	0.75	0.75	0.12	0.72	0.21	0.18	0.38	0.24
Injury Height	0.42	0.98	0.59	0.56	0.74	0.64	0.10	0.91	0.18	0.24	0.51	0.33
Injury Type	0.70	0.91	0.79	0.81	0.73	0.77	0.07	0.48	0.12	0.18	0.35	0.24
Injury Device	0.78	0.93	0.85	0.86	0.79	0.82	0.20	0.77	0.32	0.11	0.28	0.16
***Treatment* Average**	0.45	0.91	0.61	0.53	0.78	0.63	0.14	0.72	0.23	0.19	0.54	0.28
Drug	0.10	0.98	0.18	0.24	0.69	0.36	0.01	0.74	0.02	0.10	0.42	0.16
Dosage	1.00	0.81	0.90	1.00	0.76	0.86	0.30	0.52	0.38	0.32	0.46	0.38
Delivery	0.26	0.95	0.41	0.34	0.89	0.49	0.11	0.89	0.20	0.15	0.74	0.25
***Result* Average**	0.59	0.93	0.72	0.60	0.75	0.67	0.13	0.71	0.22	0.15	0.30	0.20
Investigation Method	0.29	0.96	0.45	0.27	0.79	0.40	0.03	0.66	0.06	0.02	0.16	0.04
Trend	0.37	0.91	0.53	0.44	0.78	0.56	0.06	0.63	0.11	0.07	0.27	0.11
Significance	0.70	0.90	0.79	0.70	0.71	0.70	0.17	0.69	0.27	0.22	0.39	0.28
p Value	1.00	0.96	0.98	1.00	0.71	0.83	0.27	0.86	0.41	0.30	0.36	0.33

Table 3: The macro-averaged evaluation results for each class given in precision, recall and F_1 measure.

For the *extraction* task with *all instances* setting, recall is close to 100% for all entity classes considered in the *Animal* relation. It is 81% for Dosages. The rule-based recognition for Dosages (as for Ages and p Values) is very precise: All recognized entities have been annotated by medical experts somewhere in the document. This strong difference between entity classes can be observed in the *annotation* task and the *fillers only* setting as well: The best average performance in F_1-measure is achieved for entity classes that are part of the Animal relation. Precision is best for Dosages, Ages and p Values.

The recall for the *all instances* setting is high in both the extraction and in the annotation task. However, the number of annotated instances (29,628 annotations in total) is about 25 times higher than the number of expert annotations, which leads to low precision especially in the annotation task. For the *fillers only* setting, the number of annotations decreases dramatically (to 4069 annotations); at the same time, precision improves. Regarding the comparison of both tasks, precision and recall are both notably lower in the annotation task, for the *all entities* setting, as well as for the *fillers only* setting. The overall recall is lower by 14 percentage points (pp) in the extraction task and by 26 pp in the annotation task when considering the *fillers only* setting. The decrease is most pronounced for Investigation Methods in the annotation task with a drop of 50 pp.

4.4 Discussion

The results are promising for named entity recognition. Recall is close-to-perfect in the *extraction* task and acceptable in the *annotation* task. The results for relation extraction leave space for improvement: An increase in precision can be observed but the decrease in recall is too substantial. The *Animal* relation is an exception, where an increase in F_1 measure is observed for the *fillers only* setting for nearly all entity classes, leading to 0.87 F_1 for *Animals* in the *extraction* task.

An error analysis revealed that for the *fillers only* setting, most false positives (55%) are due to the fact that the medical experts did not annotate *all* occurrences of the correct entity, but only one or a few. 18% are due to ambiguities of surface forms (for instance the abbreviation "it" for "intrathecal" leads to many false positives). Regarding false negatives, 41% are due to missing entries in our ontology database and further 26% are caused by wrong treatment of characters (mostly wrong transcriptions of characters from the PDF).

5 Conclusion and Outlook

We described the challenge of extracting relational descriptions about preclinical experiments on spinal cord injury from scientific literature. To tackle that challenge, we introduced a cascaded approach of named entity recognition, followed by relation extraction. Our results show that the first step can be achieved by relying strongly on domain-specific ontologies. We show that modeling relations as aggregated entities, and extracting them using a distance filtering principle combined with domain specific knowledge, yields promising results, specifically for the *Animal* relation.

Future work will focus on improving the recognition at the correct position in the text. This is a prerequisite to actually tackle and evaluate the relation extraction not only on the basis of detected participating entities. Therefore, improved relation detection approaches will be implemented which relax the assumption that relevant entities are found close-by in the text. In addition, we will relax the assumption that different slots of the annotation are all equally important. Finally, we will address aggregation beyond individual relations in order to allow for a fully accurate holistic assessment of experimental therapies.

Our system offers a semantic analysis of scientific papers on spinal cord injuries. This lays groundwork for populating a comprehensive semantic database on preclinical studies of SCI treatment approaches as described by Brazda et al. (2013), laying ground and supporting transfer from preclinical to clinical knowledge in the future.

References

N. Brazda, M. Kruse, F. Kruse, T. Kirchhoffer, R. Klinger, and H.-W. Müller. 2013. The CNR preclinical database for knowledge management in spinal cord injury research. *Abstracts of the Society of Neurosciences*, 148(22).

P. Buitelaar, P. Cimiano, A. Frank, M. Hartung, and S. Racioppa. 2008. Ontology-based information extraction and integration from heterogeneous data sources. *Int. J. Hum.-Comput. Stud.*, 66(11):759–788.

F. J. Damerau. 1964. A Technique for Computer Detection and Correction of Spelling Errors. *Commun. ACM*, 7(3):171–176, March.

G. Doddington, A. Mitchell, M. Przybocki, L. Ramshaw, S. Strassel, and R. Weischedel. 2004. The Automatic Content Extraction (ACE) program: tasks, data, and evaluation. In *Proceedings of LREC 2004*, pages 837–840.

A. Doms and M. Schroeder. 2005. GoPubMed: exploring PubMed with the Gene Ontology. *Nucleic Acids Res*, 33(Web Server issue):W783–W786, Jul.

D. Ferrucci and A. Lally. 2004. Building an example application with the Unstructured Information Management Architecture. *IBM Systems Journal*, 43(3):455–475.

L. Filli and M. E. Schwab. 2012. The rocky road to translation in spinal cord repair. *Ann Neurol*, 72(4):491–501.

A. Franceschini, D. Szklarczyk, S. Frankild, M. Kuhn, M. Simonovic, A. Roth, J. Lin, P. Minguez, P. Bork, C. von Mering, and L. J. Jensen. 2013. STRING v9.1: protein-protein interaction networks, with increased coverage and integration. *Nucleic Acids Res*, 41(Database issue):D808–D815, Jan.

J. Hakenberg, M. Gerner, M. Haeussler, I. Solt, C. Plake, M. Schroeder, G. Gonzalez, G. Nenadic, and C. M. Bergman. 2011. The GNAT library for local and remote gene mention normalization. *Bioinformatics*, 27(19):2769–2771, Oct.

D. Hanisch, K. Fundel, H.-T. Mevissen, R. Zimmer, and J. Fluck. 2005. ProMiner: rule-based protein and gene entity recognition. *BMC Bioinformatics*, 6 Suppl 1:S14.

M. Hofmann-Apitius, J. Fluck, L. Furlong, O. Fornes, C. Kolarik, S. Hanser, M. Boeker, S. Schulz, F. Sanz, R. Klinger, T. Mevissen, T. Gattermayer, B. Oliva, and C. M. Friedrich. 2008. Knowledge environments representing molecular entities for the virtual physiological human. *Philos Trans A Math Phys Eng Sci*, 366(1878):3091–3110, Sep.

H. Ji and R. Grishman. 2008. Refining Event Extraction through Cross-Document Inference. In *Proceedings of ACL-08: HLT*, pages 254–262, Columbus, Ohio, June. Association for Computational Linguistics.

A. Jimeno, E. Jimenez-Ruiz, V. Lee, S. Gaudan, R. Berlanga, and D. Rebholz-Schuhmann. 2008. Assessment of disease named entity recognition on a corpus of annotated sentences. *BMC Bioinformatics*, 9 Suppl 3:S3.

J. Lafferty, A. McCallum, and F. C. N. Pereira. 2001. Conditional Random Fields: Probabilistic Models for Segmenting and Labeling Sequence Data. In *Proceedings of ICML 2001*, pages 282–289. Morgan Kaufmann.

V. P. Lemmon, A. R. Ferguson, P. G. Popovich, X.-M. Xu, D. M. Snow, M. Igarashi, C. E. Beattie, J. L. Bixby et al. 2014. Minimum Information About a Spinal Cord Injury Experiment (MIASCI) – a proposed reporting standard for spinal cord injury experiments. *Neurotrauma*. in press.

C. E. Lipscomb. 2000. Medical Subject Headings (MeSH). *Bull Med Libr Assoc*, 88(3):265–266, Jul.

C. Lok. 2010. Literature mining: Speed reading. *Nature*, 463(7280):416–418, Jan.

D. Nadeau and S. Sekine. 2007. A survey of named entity recognition and classification. *Lingvisticae Investigationes*, 30(1):3–26.

C. Nedellec, R. Bossy, J.-D. Kim, J. jae Kim, T. Ohta, S. Pyysalo, and P. Zweigenbaum, editors. 2013. *Proceedings of the BioNLP Shared Task 2013 Workshop*. Association for Computational Linguistics, Sofia, Bulgaria, August.

P. V. Ogren. 2006. Knowtator: a protégé plug-in for annotated corpus construction. In *Proceedings NAACL/HLT 2006*, pages 273–275, Morristown, NJ, USA. Association for Computational Linguistics.

E. Pafilis, S. P. Frankild, L. Fanini, S. Faulwetter, C. Pavloudi, A. Vasileiadou, C. Arvanitidis, and L. J. Jensen. 2013. The SPECIES and ORGANISMS Resources for Fast and Accurate Identification of Taxonomic Names in Text. *PLoS One*, 8(6):e65390.

F. Prinz, T. Schlange, and K. Asadullah. 2011. Believe it or not: how much can we rely on published data on potential drug targets? *Nat Rev Drug Discov*, 10(9):712, Sep.

H. Saggion, A. Funk, D. Maynard, and K. Bontcheva. 2007. Ontology-Based Information Extraction for Business Intelligence. In K. A. et al., editor, *The Semantic Web*, volume 4825 of *Lecture Notes in Computer Science*, pages 843–856. Springer.

G. K. Savova, J. J. Masanz, P. V. Ogren, J. Zheng, S. Sohn, K. C. Kipper-Schuler, and C. G. Chute. 2010. Mayo clinical Text Analysis and Knowledge Extraction System (cTAKES): architecture, component evaluation and applications. *J Am Med Inform Assoc*, 17(5):507–513.

E. W. Sayers, T. Barrett, D. A. Benson, E. Bolton, S. H. Bryant, K. Canese, V. Chetvernin, D. M. Church, M. Dicuccio, S. Federhen, M. Feolo, I. M. Fingerman, L. Y. Geer, W. Helmberg, Y. Kapustin, S. Krasnov, D. Landsman, D. J. Lipman, Z. Lu, T. L. Madden, T. Madej, D. R. Maglott, A. Marchler-Bauer, V. Miller, I. Karsch-Mizrachi, J. Ostell, A. Panchenko, L. Phan, K. D. Pruitt, G. D. Schuler, E. Sequeira, S. T. Sherry, M. Shumway, K. Sirotkin, D. Slotta, A. Souvorov, G. Starchenko, T. A. Tatusova, L. Wagner, Y. Wang, W. J. Wilbur, E. Yaschenko, and J. Ye. 2012. Database resources of the National Center for Biotechnology Information. *Nucleic Acids Res*, 40(Database issue):D13–D25, Jan.

M. Schuemie, R. Jelier, and J. Kors. 2007. Peregrine: lightweight gene name normalization by dictionary lookup. In *Proceedings of the Biocreative 2 workshop 2007*, page 131–140, Madrid, Spain, April.

O. Steward, P. G. Popovich, W. D. Dietrich, and N. Kleitman. 2012. Replication and reproducibility in spinal cord injury research. *Exp Neurol*, 233(2):597–605, Feb.

S. Strassel, M. Przybocki, K. Peterson, Z. Song, and K. Maeda. 2008. Linguistic Resources and Evaluation Techniques for Evaluation of Cross-Document Automatic Content Extraction. In *Proceedings of the Language Resources and Evaluation Conference*, pages 2706–2709.

P. Thomas, J. Starlinger, A. Vowinkel, S. Arzt, and U. Leser. 2012. GeneView: a comprehensive semantic search engine for PubMed. *Nucleic Acids Res*, 40:W585–W591, Jul.

J. Tsujii, J.-D. Kim, and S. Pyysalo, editors. 2011. *Proceedings of BioNLP Shared Task 2011 Workshop*. Association for Computational Linguistics, Portland, Oregon, USA, June.

J. Tsujii, editor. 2009. *Proceedings of the BioNLP 2009 Workshop Companion Volume for Shared Task*. Association for Computational Linguistics, Boulder, Colorado, June.

D. C. Wimalasuriya and D. Dou. 2010. Ontology-based information extraction: An introduction and a survey of current approaches. *Journal of Information Science*, 36(3):306–323.

Semi-supervised Sequence Labeling for Named Entity Extraction based on Tri-Training: Case Study on Chinese Person Name Extraction

Chien-Lung Chou[1]
National Central University,
Taoyuan, Taiwan
formatc.chou@gmail.com

Chia-Hui Chang
National Central University,
Taoyuan, Taiwan
chia@csie.ncu.edu.tw

Shin-Yi Wu
Industrial Technology
Research Institute, Taiwan
sywu@itri.org.tw

Abstract

Named entity extraction is a fundamental task for many knowledge engineering applications. Existing studies rely on annotated training data, which is quite expensive when used to obtain large data sets, limiting the effectiveness of recognition. In this research, we propose an automatic labeling procedure to prepare training data from structured resources which contain known named entities. While this automatically labeled training data may contain noise, a self-testing procedure may be used as a follow-up to remove low-confidence annotation and increase the extraction performance with less training data. In addition to the preparation of labeled training data, we also employed semi-supervised learning to utilize large unlabeled training data. By modifying tri-training for sequence labeling and deriving the proper initialization, we can further improve entity extraction. In the task of Chinese personal name extraction with 364,685 sentences (8,672 news articles) and 54,449 (11,856 distinct) person names, an F-measure of 90.4% can be achieved.

1 Introduction

Detecting named entities in documents is one of the most important tasks for message understanding. For example, the #Microposts 2014 Workshop hosted an "Entity Extraction and Linking Challenge", which aimed to automatically extract entities from English microposts and link them to the corresponding English DBpedia v3.9 resources (if a linkage existed). Like many other types of research, this task relies on annotated training examples that require large amounts of manual labeling, leading to a limited number of training examples (e.g. 2.3K tweets). While human-labelled training examples (L) have high quality, their cost is very high. Thus the major concern in this paper is how to prepare training data for entity extraction learning on the Web.

In practice, sometimes there are existing structured databases of known entities that are valuable to improve extraction accuracy. For examples, personal names, school names, and company names can be obtained from a Who's Who website, and accessible government data for registered schools and businesses, respectively. Meanwhile, there are many unlabeled training examples that can be used for many information extraction tasks. If we can automatically label known entities in the unlabeled training examples, we can obtain large labeled training set. While such training data may contain errors, self-testing can be applied to filter unreliable labeling with less confidence.

On the other hand, the use of unlabeled training examples (U) has also been proved to be a promising technique for classification. For example, co-training (Blum and Mitchell, 1998) and tri-training (Zhou et al. 2005) are two successful techniques that use examples with high-confidence as predicted by the other classifier or examples with consensus answers from the other two classifiers in order to prepare new labeled training data for learning. By estimating the error rate of each learned classifier, we can calculate the maximum number of new consensus answers for learning to ensure the error rates are reduced.

In this paper, we explore the possibility of extending semi-supervised learning to sequence labeling via tri-training so that unlabeled training examples can also be used in the learning phase. The challenge here is to obtain a common label sequence as a consensus answer from multiple models. As enumerating

[1] This research was partially supported by ITRI, Taiwan under grant B2-101052.

Proceedings of Third Workshop on Semantic Web and Information Extraction, pages 33–40,
Dublin, Ireland, 24 August, 2014.

all possible label sequences will be too time-consuming, we employ a confidence level to control the co-labeling answer such that a label sequence with the largest probability is selected. Comparing with a common label sequence from multiple models, the most probable label sequence has larger chance to obtain a consensus answer for training and testing.

In addition to the extension of tri-training algorithm to sequence labeling, another key issue with tri-training is the assumption of the initial error rate (0.5), leading to a limited number of co-labeling examples for training and early termination for large set training. Therefore, a new estimation method is devised for the estimation of initial error rate to alleviate the problem and improve the overall performance.

To validate the proposed method, we conduct experiments on Chinese personal name extraction using 7,000 known Chinese celebrity names (abbreviated as CCN). We collect news articles containing these personal names from Google's search engine (using these names as keywords) and automatically label these articles containing CCN and known reporters' names. In a test set of 8,672 news articles (364,685 sentences) containing 54,449 personal names (11,856 distinct names), the basic model built on CRF (conditional random field) has a performance of 76.8% F-measure when using 500 celebrity names for preparing training data, and is improved to 86.4% F-measure when 7,000 celebrity names are used. With self-testing, the performance is improved to 88.9%. Finally, tri-training can further improve the performance through unlabeled data to 90.4%.

2 Related Work

Entity extraction is the task of recognizing named entities from unstructured text documents, which is one of the information tasks to test how well a machine can understand the messages written in natural language and automate mundane tasks normally performed by human. The development of machine learning research from classification to sequence labeling such as the HMM (Hidden Markov Model) (Bikel et al., 1997) and the CRF (Conditional Random Field) (McCallum and Wei, 2003) has been widely discussed in recent years. While supervised learning shows an impressive improvement over unsupervised learning, it requires large training data to be labeled with answers. Therefore, semi-supervised approaches are proposed.

Semi-supervised learning refers to techniques that also make use of unlabeled data for training. Many approaches have been previously proposed for semi-supervised learning, including: generative models, self-learning, co-training, graph-based methods (Zhou et al. 2005) and information-theoretic regularization (Zheng et al. 2009). In contrast, although a number of semi-supervised classifications have been proposed, semi-supervised learning for sequence segmentation has received considerably less attention and is designed according to a different philosophy.

Co-training and tri-training have been mainly discussed for classification tasks with relatively few labeled training examples. For example, the original co-training paper by Blum and Mitchell (1998) described experiments to classify web pages into two classes using only 12 labeled web pages as examples. This co-training algorithm requires two views of the training data and learns a separate classifier for each view using labeled examples. Nigam and Ghani (2000) demonstrated that co-training performed better when the independent feature set assumption is valid. For comparison, they conducted their experiments on the same (WebKB course) data set used by Blum and Mitchell.

Goldman and Zhou (2000) relaxed the redundant and independent assumption and presented an algorithm that uses two different supervised learning algorithms to learn a separate classifier from the provided labeled data. Empirical results demonstrated that two standard classifiers can be used to successfully label data for each other with 95% confidence interval.

Tri-training (Zhou, et al. 2005) was an improvement of co-training, which used three classifiers and a voting mechanism to solve the confidence issue of co-labeled answers by two classifiers. In each round of tri-training, the classifiers h_j and h_k choose some examples in U to label for h_i $(i, j, k \in \{1,2,3\}$, $i \neq j \neq k)$. Let L_i^t denote the set of examples that are labeled for h_i in the t-th round. Then the training set for h_i in the t-th round are $L \cup L_i^t$. Note that the unlabeled examples labeled in the t-th round, i.e. L_i^t, won't be put into the original labeled example set, i.e. L. Instead, in the $(t+1)$-th round all the examples in L_i^t will be regarded as unlabeled and put into U again.

While Tri-training has been used in many classification tasks, the application in sequence labeling tasks is limited. Chen et al. (2006) proposed an agreement measure that computed the unit consistency

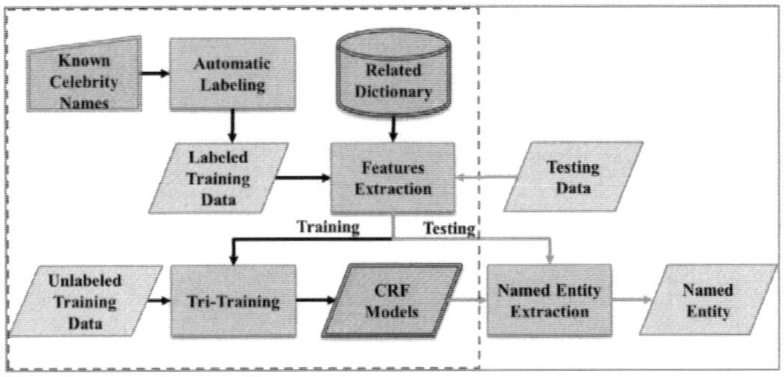

Figure 1 Semi-Supervised Named Entity Extraction Based on Automatic Labeling and Tri-training

between two label sequences from two models. Then based on the agreement measure, the idea is to choose a sentence, which is correctly labeled by h_j and h_k but is not parsed correctly by the target classifier h_i, to be a new training sample. A control parameter is used to determine the percentage (30%) of examples selected for the next round. The process iterates until no more unlabeled examples are available. Thus, Chen et al.'s method does not ensure the PAC learning theory.

3 System Architecture

Due to the high cost of labeling, most benchmarks for NER are limited to several thousand sentences. For example, the English dataset for the CoNLL 2003 shared task (Tjong et al., 2003) consists of 14,987 training sentences for four entity categories, PER, LOC, ORG, and MISC. But it is unclear whether sufficient data is provided for training or the learning algorithms have reached their capacity. Therefore, two intuitive ways are considered in this paper: one is automatic labeling of unlabeled data for preparing a large amount of annotated training examples, and the other is semi-supervised learning for making use of both labeled and unlabeled data during learning.

For the former, *automatic labeling* is sometimes possible, especially for named entities which can be obtained from Web resources like DBpedia. For example, suppose we want to train a named entity extractor for the Reuters Corpus, we can use the known entities from CoNLL 2003 shared task as queries to obtain documents that contain queries from the Reuters Corpus and label the articles automatically. While such automatic annotation may involve wrong labeling, we can apply *self-testing* to filter low-confidence labels. Overall, the benefit of the large amount of labeled training examples is greater than the noise it may cause.

In this paper, we propose a hybrid model composed of the following modules: automatic labeling, feature engineering, and tri-training based algorithm for training and testing. The framework is illustrated in Figure 1.

3.1 Tri-training for Classification

Let L denote the labeled example set with size $|L|$ and U denote the unlabeled example set with size $|U|$. In each round, t, tri-training uses two models, h_j and h_k, to label the answer of each instance x from unlabeled training data U. If h_j and h_k give the same answer, then we could use x and the common answer pair as newly training example, i.e. $L_i^t = \{(x,y): x \in U, y = h_j^t(x) = h_k^t(x)\}$) for model h_i ($i,j,k \in \{1,2,3\}$, $i \neq j \neq k$). To ensure that the error rate is reduced through iterations, when training h_i, Eq. (1) must be satisfied,

$$e_i^t|L_i^t| < e_i^{t-1}|L_i^{t-1}| \quad (1)$$

where e_i^t denotes the error rate of model h_i in L_i^t, which is estimated by h_j and h_k in the t-th round using the labeled data L by dividing the number of labeled examples on which both h_j and h_k make an incorrect estimation by the number of labeled examples for which the estimation made by h_j is the same as that made by h_k, as shown in Eq. (2).[2]

[2] Assuming that the unlabeled examples hold the same distribution as that held by the labeled ones.

$$e_i^t = \frac{|\{(x,y) \in L, h_j^t(x) = h_k^t(x) \neq y\}|}{|\{(x,y) \in L, h_j^t(x) = h_k^t(x)\}|} \tag{2}$$

If $|L_i^t|$ is too large, such that Eq. (1) is violated, it would be necessary to sample maximum u examples from L_i^t such that Eq. (1) can be satisfied.

$$u = \left\lceil \frac{e_i^{t-1}|L_i^{t-1}|}{e_i^t} - 1 \right\rceil \tag{3}$$

$$S_i^t = \begin{cases} Subsample(L_i^t, u) & violated\ Eq. (1) \\ L_i^t & otherwise \end{cases} \tag{4}$$

For the last step in each round, the union of the labeled training examples L and S_i^t, i.e. $L \cup S_i^t$, is used as training data to update classifier h_i for this iteration.

3.2 Modification for the Initialization

According to Eq. (1), the product of error rate and new training examples define an upper bound for the next iteration. Meanwhile, $|L_i^{t-1}|$ should satisfy Eq. (5) such that $|L_i^t|$ after subsampling, i.e., u, is still bigger than $|L_i^{t-1}|$.

$$|L_i^{t-1}| > \frac{e_i^t}{e_i^{t-1} - e_i^t} \tag{5}$$

In order to estimate the size of $|L_i^1|$, i.e., the number of new training examples for the first round, we need to estimate e_i^0, e_i^1, and $|L_i^0|$ first. Zhou et al. assumed a 0.5 error rate for e_i^0, computed e_i^1 by h_j and h_k, and estimated the lower bound for $|L_i^0|$ by Eq. (6), thus:

$$|L_i^0| = \left\lfloor \frac{e_i^1}{e_i^0 - e_i^1} + 1 \right\rfloor = \left\lfloor \frac{e_i^1}{0.5 - e_i^1} + 1 \right\rfloor \tag{6}$$

The problem with this initialization is that, for a larger dataset $|L|$, such an initialization will have no effect on retraining and will lead to an early stop for tri-training. For example, consider the case when the error rate e_i^1 is less than 0.4, then the value of $|L_i^0|$ will be no more than 5, leading to a small upper bound for $e_i^1|L_i^1|$ according to Eq. (1). That is to say, we can only sample a small subset $|S_i^1|$ from L_i^1 for training h_i based on Eq. (4). On the other hand, if e_i^1 is close to 0.5 such that the value of $|L_i^0|$ is greater than the original dataset $|L|$, it may completely alter the behavior of h_i.

To avoid this difficulty, we propose a new estimation for the product $e_i^0|L_i^0|$. Let $L^C(h_j, h_k)$ denote the set of labeled examples (from L) on which the classification made by h_j is the same as that made by h_k in the initial round, and $L^W(h_j, h_k)$ denote the set of examples from $L^C(h_j, h_k)$ on which both h_j and h_k make incorrect classification, as shown in Eq. (7) and (8). In addition, we define $L_i^W(h_j, h_k)$ to be the set of examples from $L^C(h_j, h_k)$ on which h_i makes incorrect classification in the initial round, as shown in Eq. (9). The relationship among $L^C(h_j, h_k)$, $L^W(h_j, h_k)$, and $L_i^W(h_j, h_k)$ is illustrated in Figure 2.

$$L^C(h_j, h_k) = \{(x, y) \in L: h_j(x) = h_k(x)\} \tag{7}$$

$$L^W(h_j, h_k) = \{(x, y) \in L^C(h_j, h_k): h_j(x) \neq y\} \tag{8}$$

$$L_i^W(h_j, h_k) = \{(x, y) \in L^C(h_j, h_k): h_i(x) \neq y\} \tag{9}$$

By replacing $e_i^0|L_i^0|$ with $L_i^W(h_j, h_k)$ and estimation of e_i^1 by $|L^W(h_j, h_k)|/|L^C(h_j, h_k)|$), we can estimate an upper bound for $|L_i^0|$ via Eq. (3). That is to say, we can compute an upper bound for $|L_i^0|$ and replace Eq. (3) by Eq. (10) to estimate the maximum data size of $|L_i^1|$, in the first round.

$$|L_i^0| = \left\lceil \frac{e_i^0|L_i^0|}{e_i^1} - 1 \right\rceil = \left\lceil \frac{L_i^W(h_j,h_k) * L^C(h_j,h_k)}{L^W(h_j,h_k)} - 1 \right\rceil \tag{10}$$

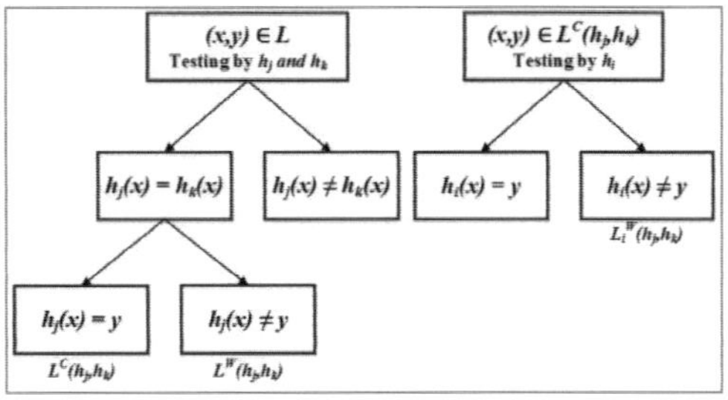

Figure 2 The relationship among Eq. (7), (8), and (9).

3.3 Modification for Co-Labeling

The tri-training algorithm was originally designed for traditional classification. For sequence labeling, we need to define what should be the common labels for the input example x when two models (training time) or three models (testing time) are involved. In Chen et al.'s work, they only consider the most probable label sequence from each model; the selection method chooses examples (for h_i) with the highest-agreement labeled sentences by h_j and h_k, and the lowest-agreement labeled sentences by h_i and h_j; finally, the newly training samples were labeled by h_j (ignoring the label result by h_k).

As the probability for two sequence labelers to output the same label sequence is low (a total of $5^{|l|}$ (BIEOS Tagging) possible label sequences with length l), we propose a different method to resolve this issue. Assume that each model can output the m best label sequences with highest probability (m=5). Let $P_i(y|x)$ denote the probability that an instance x has label y estimated by h_i. We select the label with the largest probability sum by the co-labeling models. In other words, we could use h_j and h_k to estimate possible labels, then choose the label y with the maximum probability sum, $P_j(y|x) + P_k(y|x)$, to re-train h_i. Thus, the set of examples, L_i^t, prepared for h_i in the t-th round is defined as follows:

$$L_i^t = \left\{(x, y): x \in U, \max_y(P_j(y|x) + P_k(y|x)) \geqq \theta * 2\right\} \quad (11)$$

where θ(default 0.5) is a threshold that controls the quality of the training examples provided to h_i.

During testing, the label y for an instance x is determined by three models h_1, h_2 and h_3. We choose the output with the largest probability sum from *3* models with a confidence $\theta * 3$ or $\theta * 2$. If the label with the largest probability sum from *3* models is not greater than $\theta * 3$, then we choose the one with the largest probability from single model with a maximum probability. That is to say, if the label with the largest probability sum from three models is not greater than $\theta * 3$, then we choose the one with the largest probability sum from two models with a confidence of $\theta * 2$. The last selection criterion is the label with the maximum probability estimated by the three models as shown in Eq. (12).

$$y = \max_y \begin{Bmatrix} \max_y(P_1(y|x) + P_2(y|x) + P_3(y|x)) \geq \theta * 3 \\ \max_y(P_i(y|x) + P_j(y|x)) \geq \theta * 2, i, j \in \{1,2,3\}, i \neq j \\ \max_y(P_1(y|x), P_2(y|x), P_3(y|x)) \end{Bmatrix} \quad (12)$$

4 Experiments

We apply our proposed approach on Chinese personal name extraction. We use known celebrity names to query search engines for news articles from four websites (including Liberty Times, Apple Daily, China Times, and United Daily News) and collect the top 10 search results for sentences that contain the query keyword and uses these query keyword as extraction target via automatic labeling. Given different numbers of personal names, we prepare six datasets by automatically labeling as mentioned in the beginning of Section 3 and consider them as labeled training examples. We also crawl these four news websites from 2013/01/01 to 2013/03/31 and obtain 20,974 articles for unlabeled and testing data. To increase the possibility of containing person names, we select sentences that include some common

Table 1 Labeled dataset (L) and unlabeled dataset (U) for Chinese person name extraction

	L						U
	Dataset 1	Dataset 2	Dataset 3	Dataset 4	Dataset 5	Dataset 6	--
#Names	500	1,000	2,000	3,000	5,000	7,053	--
Sentences	5,548	10,928	21,267	30,653	50,738	67,104	240,994
Words	106,535	208,383	400,111	567,794	913,516	1,188,822	4,251,861

surname followed by some common first name to obtain 240,994 as unlabeled data (U) (Table 1). For testing, we manually labeled 8,672 news articles, yielding a total of 364,685 sentences with 54,449 person names (11,856 distinct person names).

For the tagging scheme, we used BIEOS to mark the named entities to be extracted. Fourteen features were used in the experiment including, common surnames, first names, job titles, numeric tokens, alphabet tokens, punctuation symbol, and common characters in front or behind personal names. The predefined dictionaries contain 486 job titles, 224 surnames, 38,261 first names, and 107 symbols as well as 223 common words in front of and behind person name. We use CRF++ (Kudo 2004) for the following experiment. With a template involving unigram macros and the previous three tokens and behind, a total of 195 features are produced. We define precision, recall and F-measure based on the number personal names as follows:

$$Precision = \frac{Correctly\ identified\ names}{Identified\ names} \quad (13)$$

$$Recall = \frac{Correctly\ identified\ names}{Real\ names} \quad (14)$$

$$F - Measure = 2PR/(P + R) \quad (15)$$

4.1 Performance of Automatic Labeling & Self-Testing

As mentioned above, using the query keyword itself to label the collected news articles (called uni-labeling) only labels a small part of known person names. Therefore, we also use all celebrity names and six report name patterns such as "UDN [reporter name]/Taipei" (聯合報[記者名]/台北報導), to label all collected articles (called Full-labelling). While this automatic labelling procedure does not ensure perfect training data, it provides acceptable labelled training for semi-supervised learning. As shown in Figure 3, the automatic labelling procedure can greatly improve the performance on the testing data.

Based on this basic model, we apply self-testing to filter examples with low confidence and retrain a new model with the set of high confidence examples. The idea is to use the trained CRF model to test the training data themselves and output the conditional probability for the most possible label sequence. By removing examples with low confidence we can retrain a new model with the set of high confidence examples. As indicated by black-dashed line (with + symbol) in Figure 4, the F-measures increases as the data size increases. The performance of self-testing is improved for all datasets with confidence levels from 0.5 to 0.9. An F-measure of 0.815 (Dataset 1) to 0.889 (Dataset 6) can be obtained, depending on the number of celebrity names we have. The best performance is achieved at confidence level 0.8 for all data sets except for dataset 3 which has the best performance when T = 0.9.

4.2 Performance of Tri-Training

Next, we evaluate the effect of using unlabeled training data based on tri-training. In our initial attempt to apply original tri-training, we obtained no improvement for all datasets. As shown in Figure 5, the final data size used for training and the performance is similar to those values obtained for the self-testing results (with confidence level 0.8). This is because we have a very small estimation of $|L_i^0|$ by Eq. (6) when a 0.5 initial error rate for e_i^0 (i∈{1,2,3}) is assumed. Therefore, it does not make any improvement on retraining.

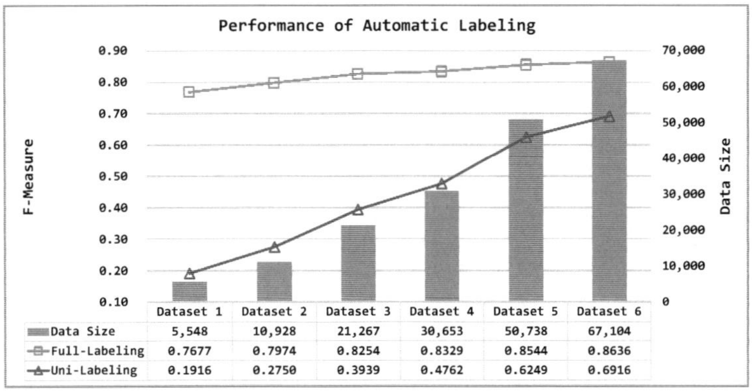

Figure 3 Performance Comparison of automatic labeling

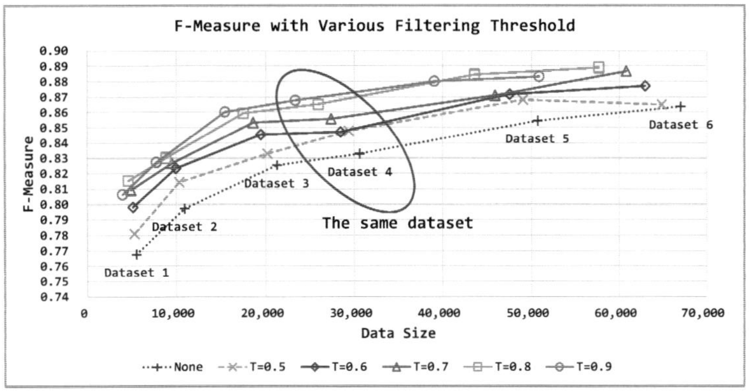

Figure 4 Performance Comparison of self-testing

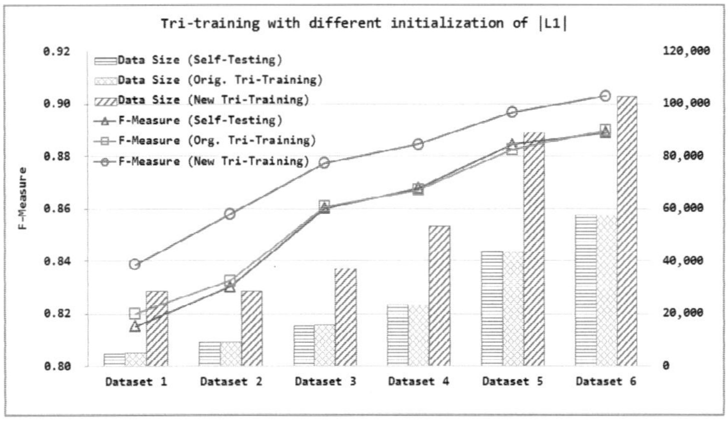

Figure 5 Performance of Tri-training with different initialization for $|L^1|$

However, with the new initialization by Eq. (10), the number of examples that can be sampled from unlabeled dataset $|L_i^1|$ is greatly increased. For dataset 1, the unlabeled data selected is five times the original data size (an increase from 4,637 to 25,234), leading to an improvement of 2.4% in F-measure (from 0.815 to 0.839). For dataset 2, the final data size is twice the original data size (from 8,881 to 26,173) with an F-measure improvement of 2.7% (from 0.830 to 0.857). For dataset 6, since $|L_i^1|$ is too large to be loaded for training with L, we only use 75% for experiment. The improvement in F-measure is 1.5%. Overall, an improvement of 1.2% ~ 2.7% can be obtained with this tri-training algorithm.

5 Conclusion

Named entity extraction has been approached with supervised approaches that require large labeled training examples to achieve good performance. This research makes use of automatic labeling based on known entity names to create a large corpus of labeled training data. While such data may contain noise, the benefit with large labeled training data still is more significant than noise it inherits. In practice, we might have a large amount of unlabeled data. Therefore, we applied tri-training to make use of such unlabeled data and to modify the co-labeling mechanism for sequence labeling to improve the performance. Instead of assuming a constant error rate for the initial error of each classifier, we proposed a new way to estimate the number of examples selected from unlabeled data. As shown in the experiments, such a semi-supervised approach can further improve the F-measure to 0.904 for dataset 6 with 7,000 celebrity names.

Reference

Rie Kubota Ando and Tong Zhang. 2005. A high-performance semi-supervised learning method for text chunking. In Proceedings of the 43rd Annual Meeting on Association for Computational Linguistics (ACL '05). pp.1-9.

Avrim Blum and Tom Mitchell. 1998. Combining labeled and unlabeled data with co-training. COLT' 98 Proceedings of the eleventh annual conference on Computational learning theory, pp. 92-100.

Wenliang Chen, Yujie Zhang and Hitoshi Isahara. Chinese Chunking with Tri-training Learning, The 21st International Conference on the Computer Processing of Oriental Languages (ICCPOL2006), LNCS, Vol. 4285, Springer, pp. 466-473, Singapore, Dec. 2006.

Sally Goldman and Yan Zhou. 2000. Enhancing supervised learning with unlabeled data. ICML'00 Proceedings of the 17th International Conference on Machine Learning, pp. 327-334.

Feng Jiao, Shaojun Wang, Chi-Hoon Lee, Russell Greiner, and Dale Schuurmans. 2006. Semi-supervised conditional random fields for improved sequence segmentation and labeling. In Proceedings of the 21st International Conference on Computational Linguistics and the 44th annual meeting of the Association for Computational Linguistics (ACL-44), pp. 209-216.

Taku Kudo. CRF++: Yet Another CRF toolkit. http://crfpp.googlecode.com/svn/trunk/doc/index.html

Wei Li, and Andrew McCallum. 2005. Semi-supervised sequence modeling with syntactic topic models. In Proceedings of the National Conference on Artificial Intelligence - Volume 2 (AAAI '05), pp. 813-818.

Gideon S. Mann and Andrew McCallum. 2010. Generalized expectation criteria for semi-supervised learning with weakly labeled data. Journal of machine learning research, Volume 11, pp.955-984.

Andrew McCallum and Wei Li. 2003. Early results for named entity recognition with conditional random fields, feature induction and web-enhanced lexicons. In Proceedings of the seventh conference on Natural language learning at HLT-NAACL 2003 - Volume 4 (CONLL '03), pp. 188-191.

Kamal Nigam and Rayid Ghani. 2000. Analyzing the effectiveness and applicability of co-training. CIKM '00 Proceedings of the ninth international conference on Information and knowledge management, pp. 86-93.

Cícero Nogueira dos Santos, Ruy Luiz Milidiú. 2012. Named entity recognition. Entropy Guided Transformation Learning: Algorithms and Applications, Springer, Briefs in Computer Science, pp. 51-58.

Erik F. Tjong, Kim Sang and Fien De Meulder. 2003. Introduction to the CoNLL-2003 shared task: language-independent named entity recognition. In Proceedings of the seventh conference on Natural language learning at HLT-NAACL 2003 - Volume 4 (CONLL '03), pp. 142-147.

Lei Zheng, Shaojun Wang, Yan Liu, and Chi-Hoon Lee. 2009. Information theoretic regularization for semi-supervised boosting. In Proceedings of the 15th ACM SIGKDD international conference on Knowledge discovery and data mining (KDD '09), pp. 1017-1026.

Dengyong Zhou, Jiayuan Huang, and Bernhard Schölkopf. 2005. Learning from labeled and unlabeled data on a directed graph. In Proceedings of the 22nd international conference on Machine learning (ICML '05), pp. 1036-1043.

Zhi-Hua Zhou and Ming Li. 2005. Tri-Training: Exploiting Unlabeled Data Using Three Classifiers. IEEE Transactions on Knowledge and Data Engineering archive, Volume 17 Issue 11, pp. 1529-1541.

Towards a robust framework for the semantic representation of temporal expressions in cultural legacy data

Daniel Isemann
Natural Language Processing Group
Department of Computer Science
Leipzig University
lastname@informatik.uni-leipzig.de

Gerard Lynch
Centre for Applied Data Analytics Research
University College Dublin
Clonskeagh, Dublin 4
Ireland

Raffaella Lanino
Documentation and Digitisation
National Gallery of Ireland
Dublin
rlanino@ngi.ie

firstname.lastname@ucd.ie

Abstract

Date and time descriptors play an important role in cultural record keeping. As part of digital access and information retrieval on heritage databases it is becoming increasingly important that date descriptors are not matched as strings but that their semantics are properly understood and interpreted by man and machine alike. This paper describes a prototype system designed to resolve temporal expressions from English language cultural heritage records to ISO 8601 compatible date expressions. The architecture we advocate calls for a two stage resolution with a "semantic layer" between the input and ISO 8601 output. The system is inspired by a similar system for German language records and was tested on real world data from the National Gallery of Ireland in Dublin. Results from an evaluation with two senior art and metadata experts from the gallery are reported.

1 Introduction

Preserving a memory of past events has been central to human culture for millennia and may even be seen as a defining element of cultural life in general. The practice of specifying locations in time for this purpose transcends cultural boundaries. The earliest precursors of the Chinese lunisolar calendar can be traced back to the second millennium before Christ. In ancient Attica the "eponymous archon" lent his name to the year he ruled in and a similar system was employed by republican Romans. The introduction of the Julian calendar and its Georgian reform, although haphazardly adopted, has eventually led to a widely accepted standard for locating events in time (although alternative calendars exist and thrive to this day). The advent of the computer age has brought with it stricter requirements for such standards, for instance that of unambiguous machine readability. A number of such standards for encoding the meaning or extension of temporal expressions have emerged in recent years (ISO 8601, TimeML, VRA core). However, legacy records in the field of cultural heritage still abound with natural language descriptions of dates and date ranges that are not expressed in a standardised form, such as "around 1660", "late 15th century", "1720-30 (?)". The non-standard nature of such expressions is compounded by inherent uncertainty about the dates which is expressed through uncertainty markers such as "around", "(?)" or similar. While human experts have little difficulty interpreting such expressions these are not amenable to machine-based processing and thus are not directly useful for querying databases based on dates, for instance. The latter purpose is much better served by date ranges with a clear beginning and end.

We argue for conceptually splitting the process of "translating", "converting" or otherwise associating informal descriptions of dates with concrete date ranges with an unambiguous beginning and end. A first step should capture the semantics of the original expression including possible uncertainty markers with as little loss in meaning as possible.[1] The target of this step should be a language independent ontology or semantic standard, such as the VRA core 4.0 date element. A second step should then map from a

[1] What we mean by minimising "loss in meaning" is essentially that in a first step uncertainty markers should be kept (albeit in a standardized form) rather then resolved to a date range (i.e. "c.1888" → "c(1888)" instead of "c.1888" → "1878-1898").

Proceedings of Third Workshop on Semantic Web and Information Extraction, pages 41–50,
Dublin, Ireland, 24 August, 2014.

representation in the semantic standard to a date range with concrete beginning and end according to user, institution or context specific preferences, using intelligent defaults in the absence of preferences.

In this paper we describe a prototype system designed to resolve temporal expressions from English language cultural heritage records to ISO 8601 compatible date expressions. The system is inspired by a similar system for German language records and was tested on real life data from the National Gallery of Ireland in Dublin and evaluated by two senior art and metadata experts from the gallery. The default rules for converting the "meaning" of date expressions to date ranges were found to be superior to the heuristics currently configured by the National Gallery in their collection management system.

2 Background

The National Gallery of Ireland (NGI) has developed a set of in-house standards for cataloguing date expressions related to the creation of artworks (Appendix A and B). These standards complement the editorial guidelines outlined in the NGI house style guide for works of art in the collection and they must be applied when entering the data into the relevant field on TMS[2] (The Museum System), the collection management system used by the Gallery. These guidelines have been created based on best practice standards for cataloguing date expressions. There are several authoritative resources that institutions can consult to draft their own in house cataloguing standards, including date format and epoch descriptors: AAT[3] (Art & Architecture Thesaurus), CDWA[4] (Categories for the Description of Works of Art) or the AAE Style Guide[5] (Association of Art Editors Style Guide), to mention just a few.

As shown in Appendix A and B, the NGI standards cover a diverse set of date expressions, from specific dates to more generic ones, giving the opportunity to enter into the system a range of years, decades or centuries. The date values are expressed as four digit years. More specific dates related to other events connected to the creation of the art work (for example for published volumes or different print editions), are recorded in the 'Historical Dates field' where the required date can be selected from a pop up calendar and the type of date can be selected from a drop down list (for example 'Published').

The Date label on TMS consists of three main fields: *Date*, which displays the actual date or range of dates related to the creation of the art work and which appears on the main object record screen as part of the basic object tombstone information; *Begin Date* and *End Date*, which represent the earliest and the latest possible years from a range of dates during which the artwork was created (Fig. 1). The Begin Date and End Date are not displayed in the Date label on the data entry screen of a record, as they are used for indexing and searching purposes only. Through the Simple Search and the Advanced Search functionality in the system it is possible to retrieve records with a range of dates, by either searching for earliest date, latest date or a certain time between these dates, the resulting records being drawn from the values recorded in the Begin and End Date.

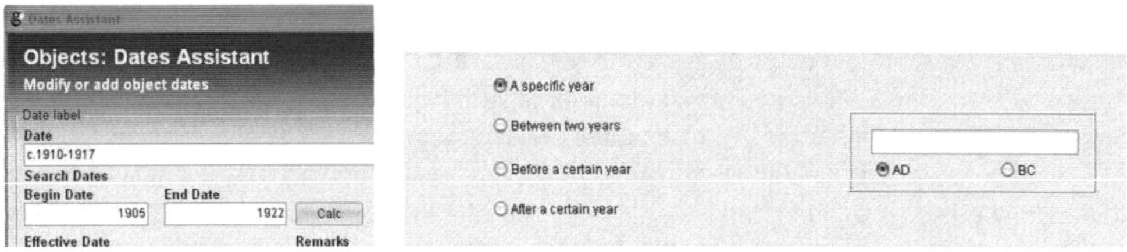

(a) "Dates Assitant" for entering dates.

(b) Panel for date queries.

Figure 1: The "Dates Assistant" for entering dates into the database and a selection panel for date queries currently in use in the collection management system of the National Gallery of Ireland.

[2] `http://www.gallerysystems.com/tms` (last accessed 13/07/2014).

[3] `http://www.getty.edu/research/tools/vocabularies/guidelines/aat_4_2_appendix_b_dates.html` (last accessed 13/07/2014).

[4] `http://www.getty.edu/research/publications/electronic_publications/cdwa/14creation.html#CREATION-DATE` (last accessed 13/07/2014).

[5] `http://www.artedit.org/styleguide.htm` (last accessed 13/07/2014).

The Begin and End Dates can be inserted automatically by the system either by pressing the 'Calc' button or by accepting a suggestion for both Begin Date and End Date which is updated automatically every time a new value is inserted in the Date field. The suggestions can be accepted or modified manually and then saved. A date expression can also be suggested by the system when entering the relevant years directly into Begin and End Date. In this case the 'Calc' button prompts a pop up window with different date expressions based on the years inserted as beginning and end. For example, by entering '1575' and '1578' in the Begin and End Date, the suggestion box for the Date field will list the following options: '1575-1578'; 'c.1576'; 'late 16th century'. When date ranges include two specific years (for example in the case of 'YYYY/YYYY' or 'YYYY-YYYY') the two year values are automatically suggested in the Begin and End Date fields. When a single year is inserted in the Date field, the Begin and End Date are automatically filled with that same year value.

Through the configuration menu it is possible to specify the range of years to be 'suggested' in the Begin and End Date when entering a particular date expression in the Date field. By default this applies for the circa label (in the NGI case the range is 5 years before and after the specified date) and decades.

Although the automatic suggestions for Begin and End Date are configurable through the back end of the system, manual input is still necessary for accuracy when entering certain date expressions. Centuries for example (in all their formats, from 'xxth century' to 'early/mid/late xxth century') are not recognized by Begin and End Date, which in these cases need to be filled in manually. However the process works in reverse: when inserting the correct earliest and latest year that indicate a century span, the suggestion box for the Date field displays different options, including the correct 'xxth century' format.

On the other hand, in the case of decades, the relevant Begin Date and End Date are correctly suggested when inserting the 'YYYYs' format in the Date field, while, when entering the relevant years indicating the time span of a decade in the Begin and End date, the options listed as suggestions for the Date field do not include the correct format, giving instead the option of selecting 'YYYY-YYYY' as an alternative.

Similarly the Date field does not distinguish between years separated by an 'or', a dash or a hyphen when displaying the suggestions based on years inserted in Begin and End Date: when two different years are inserted in the Begin and End Date, the only relevant option listed by the system is the range of years separated by a hyphen. However, when entering the same date expressions in the Date field whether separated by 'or', dash or hyphen, the correct values are inserted in the Begin and End Date.

As the Date field is a free-text field on TMS, the process of manually entering date values, especially the ones that indicate uncertainty and include a prefix and non-numerical values, gives more room for error. In addition to this, not every date expression inserted in the Date field is recognised by the Begin and End Dates, in which case these also have to be entered manually.

At the same time the automatic suggestions given for the Date field when entering Begin Date and End seem to be more comprehensive and work better and they are helpful in giving the opportunity to select the correct option without having to manually enter the data, thus reducing the possibility of error. In the case of the NGI some configuration is further needed to make the most of the automated system already in place. In particular it would be useful to include in the provided suggestions for the Begin and End Date, those date expressions that are not currently recognised by the system.

3 Methodology and data set

The development of our system is inspired by an earlier system of temporal expression resolution for German language date expressions, an auxiliary part of a research project concerned with information retrieval on digital repositories of works of art, (Isemann and Ahmad, 2014). The approach was an iterative development cycle of successively resolving ever more complex date and time descriptors and mapping them to unambiguous time spans in ISO 8601 format. The data used were German date entries in a commercially available digital collection of 40,000 works of art.[6] Example expressions from this data set are: "1707-1712", "1734/39", "1790-3", "12./13. Jh.", "1. Drittel 16. Jh.", "1420-1375 v. Chr.".

These examples represent date ranges that have a fairly well defined beginning and end. One may perhaps argue whether the 13th century should include the year 1300 or not, but in general the intended

[6]The DVD collection "40000 Meisterwerke", published by Directmedia Publishing.

boundaries are reasonably clear. The following examples, however, are compounded by the fact that they contain uncertainty markers which leave the precise date range that should be assigned to them up to context and interpretation: "um 1568", "1642 (?)", "Vor 1650", "ab 1486", "nach 1776-77".

For the experiments presented here, we obtained a similar although much smaller English language data set from the National Gallery of Ireland. The data consisted of 939 records from the NGI database, comprising date expressions such as "1791 to 1794", "1870/72", "1740s", "18th century", "1st February 1751", "?c.1893", "after 1752", "late 16th century", "mid-1930s". Unlike in the German data set, most date expressions in the NGI data are already associated with a 'Begin Date' and 'End Date' either calculated by the NGI collection management system or manually entered by NGI staff (compare Section 2). These date ranges sanctioned by art experts present a valuable additional resource which may serve as training data for statistical learning or as a benchmark to compare against.

In contrast to the German language system we are conceptually using a two stage approach in which we first attempt to represent the intended meaning of a date expression ('intension') and only then map it to a date range for search and retrieval (one might call this range the 'extension' of a date expression). For the representation of date expression semantics (intension) we have chosen the VRA core 4.0 set of metadata elements and here in particular the 'date' element.[7] VRA core is a set of categories defined and maintained by the Data Standards Committee of the Visual Resources Association.[8] The latest version 4.0 dates from 2007. The standard has been used for semantic annotation (cf. Hollink et al. (2003) which use VRA core 3.0) and defines mappings to other metadata schemata, such as Dublin Core,[9] CDWA,[10] CCO[11] (Cataloging Cultural Objects) and its own predecessors (VRA core 2.0 and 3.0). As value ranges the standard recommends widely used thesauri (AAT[12]) or controlled vocabularies (ULAN[13]) or in the case of dates the ISO 8601 standard. Structurally, the standard prescribes that 'date' elements have a 'type' attribute (such as 'creation', 'design', 'alteration') and may have an 'earliestDate' and 'latestDate' subelement, both of which should only take ISO 8601 compatible values and can be modified by a boolean 'circa' attribute.

The semantic representation is the point of departure for the resolution of a date expression to a concrete date range. This leaves room for interpretation, especially in cases where a 'circa' flag is present. Ideally this mapping should be governed by preferences at the user and/or institution level (similar to the guidelines presented in Appendices A and B).

While the interpretation of these dates may vary on a case-by-case basis and even experts may disagree, we believe that certain default rules will allow at least a rough approximation of the intended time range in many cases. Analysing the data we noticed that mentions of years are not uniformly distributed in terms of the digit they end on. Figure 2 shows the relative frequency of year end digits for the German data set (red line) in expressions involving a 'circa' flag (German: "um"). Assuming a uniform distribution of years the frequencies should be 801.1 throughout. It is statistically extremely unlikely that the observed deviation from a uniform distribution is due to chance variation (chi squared test, 9 degrees of freedom, $p < 0.001$). As it appears equally unlikely that artists over the centuries have had a particular propensity to be more productive in years ending in 0 and 5, we believe that the natural explanation is that art historians documenting temporality tend to gravitate to "round" numbers in cases of greater uncertainty. As an upshot we would like to suggest that all else being equal approximate dates involving years should be seen as less certain if they end in 0 or 5 than if they end in other digits. Accordingly we add ± 10 years to years ending in "0", ± 5 to years ending in "5" and ± 1 to years ending in other digits. Table 1 shows a number of the resolutions our system can perform.

[7] `http://www.loc.gov/standards/vracore/` (last accessed 13/07/2014).
[8] `http://www.vraweb.org` (last accessed 13/07/2013)
[9] `http://dublincore.org` (last accessed 13/07/2014).
[10] Categories for the Description of Works of Art, cf. Section 2
[11] `http://vraweb.org/ccoweb/cco/intro.html` (last accessed 13/07/2014).
[12] `http://www.getty.edu/research/tools/vocabularies/aat` (last accessed 13/07/2014).
[13] `http://www.getty.edu/research/tools/vocabularies/ulan` (last accessed 13/07/2014).

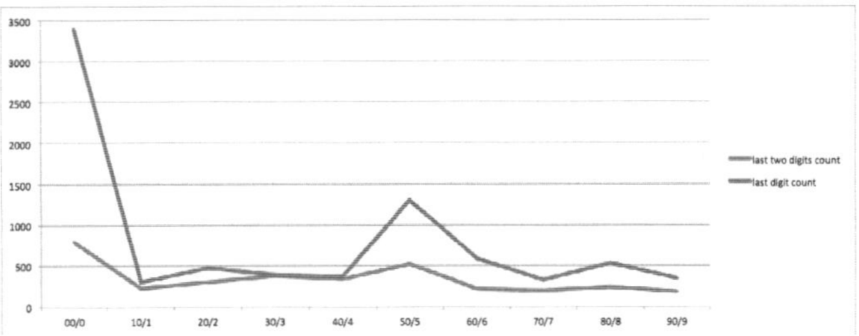

Figure 2: Distribution of year end digits in German expressions with an uncertainty marker ("um", red line) and frequencies of "00" endings compared to other multiples of 10 (blue line).

Date expression	Date resolution
1889	+1889/+1889
1522/1523	+1522/+1523
1791 to 1794	+1791/+1794
1870/72	+1870/+1872
1740s	+1740/+1749
18th century	+1700/+1799
1st February 1751	+1751/+1751

(a) Dates with well defined scope.

Date expression	Date semantics	Date resolution
c.1824	c(+1824)/c(+1824)	+1823/+1825
c.1795	c(+1795)/c(+1795)	+1790/1800
c.1890	c(+1890)/c(+1890)	+1880/+1900
?c.1893	c(+1893)/c(+1893)	+1892/+1894
after 1752	+1752/null	+1752/+1762
late 16th century	+1566/+1599	+1566/+1599
mid-1930s	+1933/+1936	+1933/+1936

(b) Dates with fuzzy scope.

Table 1: Date expressions from the National Gallery data set with default resolutions from our system. For the case of date expressions containing uncertainty or "fuzziness" we also show the semantic layer (b). Here "c(·)" represents a positive *circa* attribute in the VRA core *earliestDate* and *latestDate* subelements. Note, that not all expressions which may informally appear vague involve a *circa* attribute and that we assign a latest date by default for cases such as "after 1752", contrary to the VRA core recommendation (which we adopt as semantic representation for such cases).

4 Experiments

We implemented a rule-based date expression resolver for the expressions in the English language National Gallery data set (achieving nearly complete coverage) with the set of heuristics outlined in the previous section (cf. Table 1). Two art history and meta data experts from the National Gallery agreed to participate in an evaluation of the output of our resolution system compared against the current date range entry in the National Gallery database. The entries in the NGI database are not a direct feature of the collection management system, but rather of how the system is currently used.

We observed that our system output agreed with the NGI entries in about half of the cases (58%). In order not to burden our volunteers' time too much we did not evaluate on the complete data set, but on a randomly extracted subset in which we only included cases where our system output differed from the existing gallery records. We used a random number generator in Java to extract records until we reached a limit of 50 cases in which the two date interpretations were different. This limit was reached after selecting a total of 104 entries. The 50 non-trivial cases were compiled into a list comprised of the original date expression and a choice of two different date ranges each, one from the NGI records and one from our system. The order of the choices was randomized independently for each individual record.

The two evaluation participants were given this list together with a short introductory text outlining the background and purpose of the evaluation. They were then instructed to select which of the two date range alternatives they felt best captured the meaning of the date expression or indicate that they had no preference. Introductory paragraphs in the evaluation stressed that while individual context may sometimes enter into such a decision, they should think of the given date expressions as generic examples.

5 Results

Of the 100 individual decisions made by our two experts (50 each) exactly half (50) were in favour of our system's default recommendation, less than a third were in favour of the existing database entry (29) and just over one in five (21) had no particular preference (Table 2).

		Annotator A			
		Our System	Gallery Records	No Preference	Total Annotator B
Annotator B	Our System	8	0	3	11
	Gallery Records	19	2	6	27
	No Preference	12	0	0	12
	Total Annotator A	39	2	9	

Table 2: Agreement of preferences expressed by our evaluators in 50 test cases.

While this may be seen as an encouraging result for our date range recommender system it has to be said that in their overall preference our two evaluators were leaning different ways. While one overwhelmingly agreed with our system recommendations (preferring the NGI alternative in just two cases with nine ties), the other was leaning towards the NGI records (preferring our system in just eleven cases with twelve ties). Overall the two evaluators agreed in ten of the 50 cases (Cohen's kappa = -0.048).

We believe that the reason for the differing opinions between our two evaluators may be that one of them is working closely with the NGI database and is therefore very familiar with the status quo, including certain agreed in-house standards. The other evaluator, who was leaning towards the rules implemented in our system, is from the curatorial department and concerned with absolute and relative dating of works of art in a more theoretical way. A more thorough evaluation is needed in order to determine if the more flexible rules we are advocating would be appreciated by an expert user community.

6 Related Work

The resolution of temporal expressions is an important topic in the information extraction and semantic web community and employing these methods on cultural heritage texts in particular has been the focus of research spanning these fields and the emergent discipline of digital humanities.

Context-free grammars (CFG) for the resolution of temporal expressions have been employed by Angeli et al. (2012) and Kauppinen et al. (2010). Angeli et al. (2012) attempt to learn a probabilistic CFG for time and date expressions and at the same time an expectation maximation framework for the resolution of pragmatic ambiguity in time expressions (e.g. 'Friday' may refer to last or next Friday, 'last Friday' may refer to the previous Friday or the Friday two weeks ago etc.). For training their system they employ the TempEval-2 Task A dataset.[14] Despite the relatively small training set (1052 time expressions) they report comparable performance of their system with leading rule-based temporal resolvers.

Kauppinen et al. (2010) employ fuzzy sets towards the representation and querying of temporally disputable periodic expressions from cultural heritage such as 'late-Roman-era', 'Middle Ages' or 'beginning of the 1st century BC', which can vary due to subjectivity or lack of hard records. They define a date span with a fuzzy beginning and end which encompasses the widest possible bounds for a temporal period and then a more concise beginning and end which encompasses more constrained bounds. Queries are matched against the fuzzy set using a bespoke querying model which finds the level of overlap between the query and the fuzzy set. They test their theories on a set of records from the Ancient Milan[15] project, representing fuzzy date ranges as four RDF triples, one for each of the date points. They represent definite temporal expressions such as *First half of the 1st Century BC* in Backus-Naur form.

Research into frameworks for temporal expression extraction in the computational sciences, (Chang and Manning (2012), Strötgen and Gertz (2010), Sun et al. (2013)) has tended to focus on domains such as clinical texts and newswire for developing temporal expression resolution systems. We believe, however, that there is a clear and present need for systems and frameworks which can extract structured information from cultural heritage text, particularly in the domain of fine art image catalogues. These methodologies can enable the development of smarter retrieval systems for catalogues of cultural history

[14]Cf. `http://timeml.org/tempeval2` (last accessed 13/07/2014).

[15]`http://www.csai.disco.unimib.it/CSAI/space/CuRM/projects+and+research/Milano+Antica` (last accessed 13/07/2014).

data. Grandi and Mandreoli (2001), Grandi (2002) describe work on representing a geographical history resource, *il Dizionario geografico, fisico e storico della Toscana*[16] created by cultural historian Emanuele Repetti in the early 19th century. They focus on the resolution of temporal expressions' indeterminancy and varying granularity in Italian temporal expressions, such as *around X*, *circa. X*, *near the end of the X century* and others. They represent such indeterminacy using a four category classification of date expressions and a *probabilistic* approach from the TSQL2 standard, (Snodgrass et al. (1994)). Lilis and others (2005) use multidimensional RDF in their representation of cultural artifacts in a museum setting.

Smith (2002) focuses on detecting events in unstructured historical text with dates forming the main focus of his study. The author investigates the co-occurrence of place names and dates in 19th century text and extracts a geo-located list of events from the text. He mentions that 98% of numerical tokens in the texts refer to dates, although in different text genres, date information may be more vaguely expressed. Furthermore, he finds that certain dates are expressed as a calendar day and others refer merely to the year an event occurred. These expressions can prove problematic for traditional date processing algorithms, and often a more complex mapping is required to convert these textual representations to a computational formalism such as the CIDOC specification. Chang and Manning (2012) focus on generic temporal expressions with their SUTIME parser, which represents date and temporal information extracted from text using the TIMEX3 tag format from the TimeML (Boguraev and Ando (2005)) standard.

An emerging trend in date resolution literature encompasses the *big data* paradigm. Blamey et al. (2013) develop a probabilistic approach toward modelling everyday natural language date expressions[17] using textual data from image descriptions and EXIF[18] data from uploaded photos on the flickr website.

7 Conclusion and Future Work

We have presented and tested a system specifically designed for the resolution of date expressions in cultural heritage legacy records and we have argued for a 'semantic layer' between the literal expressions and the date range resolution. Our evaluation, although small scale, suggests that such a system may potentially be able to improve even records which already incorporate date resolutions, if slightly more complex rules than are contained in the current system or data entry guidelines are implemented.

A number of possible lines of future work suggest themselves. In order to arrive at an explicit local grammar for 'heritage dates' (cf. Kauppinen et al. (2010) and Angeli et al. (2012)), we have created a context-free grammar, that accepts roughly the same input as our current rule set. Initial examination suggests that the non-lexical part of the grammar can cover both English and German language data given appropriate lexicons. The grammar phrases can be mapped to representations in the semantic layer thereby in effect creating a system which could process multilingual input and produce consistent output.

A further extension to the system would involve the processing of semantically more complex temporal period expressions, such as "Victorian", "Edwardian", "Gründerzeit", "Gilded Age" or "Renaissance". Examples tied to the reign of a monarch tend towards a more defined scope however wider-ranging and more culturally-disputed periods such as "the Renaissance" tend to attract a less precise beginning and end-date than the former examples and may require a more complex set of semantics. Data-driven approaches could be employed to model the temporal boundaries for temporal expressions of a more vague nature. Angeli et al. (2012) demonstrate that this may be feasible even on relatively small datasets.

Examples which could benefit from an ontological augmentation involving events and periods include the practice of dating works of art with implicit reference to such periods based on a believed or previously confirmed date for a major event such as a battle or war. One example of this practice could be an artwork dated "after 1453", with the date actually representing the current dating of the fall of Constantinople. As historical information is updated or revised, the corresponding date range estimating the temporal origin of a work could be resolved based on updated information for the reference event. Similar suggestions were made in (Isemann and Ahmad, 2009). Perhaps the practically most relevant example of this kind could be cross-referencing the lifespan of an artist associated with the production

[16] A geographical, physical and historical dictionary of Tuscany

[17] Their work focuses on UK-specific cultural expressions such as Bonfire Night, first day of summer, Christmas holidays.

[18] Timestamps saved by digital cameras.

of a work with the temporal expression for its creation: if the expression says “after 1756” but we have concrete knowledge that the artist died in 1758, this can be used to add bounds to the creation event.

Acknowledgements

The authors would like to thank Dr Adriaan Waiboer, curator for Northern European Art at the National Gallery of Ireland, for valuable suggestions and his help in organising the expert evaluation.

References

Gabor Angeli, Christopher Manning, and Daniel Jurafsky. 2012. Parsing time: Learning to interpret time expressions. In *Proceedings of the 2012 Conference of the North American Chapter of the Association for Computational Linguistics: Human Language Technologies*, pages 446–455, Montréal, Canada, June. Association for Computational Linguistics.

Ben Blamey, Tom Crick, and Giles Oatley. 2013. 'The First Day of Summer': Parsing temporal expressions with distributed semantics. In *Research and Development in Intelligent Systems XXX*, pages 389–402. Springer International Publishing.

Branimir Boguraev and Rie Kubota Ando. 2005. Timeml-compliant text analysis for temporal reasoning. In *Proceedings of the 19th international joint conference on Artificial intelligence*, pages 997–1003. Morgan Kaufmann Publishers Inc.

Angel X Chang and Christopher Manning. 2012. Sutime: A library for recognizing and normalizing time expressions. In *LREC*, pages 3735–3740.

Fabio Grandi and Federica Mandreoli. 2001. The "XML/Repetti" Project: Encoding and Manipulation of Temporal Information in Historical Text Sources. In *ICHIM (2)*, pages 243–252. Citeseer.

Fabio Grandi. 2002. Xml representation and management of temporal information for web-based cultural heritage applications. *Data Science Journal*, 1(1):68–83.

L. Hollink, A. Th. Schreiber, B. Wielemaker, and B. Wielinga. 2003. Semantic annotation of image collections. In *Proceedings of the KCAP'03 Workshop on Knowledge Markup and Semantic Annotation*, Florida, USA, October.

Daniel Isemann and Khurshid Ahmad. 2009. Navigating cultural heritage in style. Sketching an ontological representation of metadata: the example of artistic period and style. *Museum Ireland*, 19:149–155.

Daniel Isemann and Khurshid Ahmad. 2014. Ontological access to images of fine art. *Journal on Computing and Cultural Heritage (JOCCH)*, 7(1):3.

Tomi Kauppinen, Glauco Mantegari, Panu Paakkarinen, Heini Kuittinen, Eero Hyvönen, and Stefania Bandini. 2010. Determining relevance of imprecise temporal intervals for cultural heritage information retrieval. *International journal of human-computer studies*, 68(9):549–560.

Pantelis Lilis et al. 2005. A metadata model for representing time-dependent information in cultural collections. In *MTSR, First online metadata and semantics research conference, Conference Proceedings*. Citeseer.

David A. Smith. 2002. Detecting and browsing events in unstructured text. In *Proceedings of the 25th Annual International ACM SIGIR Conference on Research and Development in Information Retrieval*, SIGIR '02, pages 73–80, New York, NY, USA. ACM.

Richard Thomas Snodgrass, Ilsoo Ahn, Gad Ariav, Don S Batory, James Clifford, Curtis E Dyreson, Ramez Elmasri, Fabio Grandi, Christian S Jensen, Wolfgang Käfer, et al. 1994. Tsql2 language specification. *Sigmod Record*, 23(1):65–86.

Jannik Strötgen and Michael Gertz. 2010. Heideltime: High quality rule-based extraction and normalization of temporal expressions. In *Proceedings of the 5th International Workshop on Semantic Evaluation*, SemEval '10, pages 321–324, Stroudsburg, PA, USA. Association for Computational Linguistics.

Weiyi Sun, Anna Rumshisky, and Ozlem Uzuner. 2013. Evaluating temporal relations in clinical text: 2012 i2b2 challenge. *Journal of the American Medical Informatics Association*, 20(5):806–813.

A NGI definitions/explanations of date expressions

Rules for object date

Date	Definition
1513	executed in 1513
c.1513	executed sometime around 1513 (for the purposes of search dates in TMS this will be 5 years either side e.g. begin 1508, end 1518)
1513-1515	begun in 1513, finished in 1515
1513/1516	executed sometime around the years 1513 to 1516
1513 or 1515	executed in either 1513 or 1515

Do not use c. (for circa) with a / (slash).

Figure 3: Rules for interpreting object date descriptions in NGI records.

B NGI guidelines for entering dates and date ranges

	Display Date	Search Date Begin	Search Date End	Rule
Single date	1855	1855	1855	
Begin date and end date (begun 1630, finished 1633)	1630-1633	1630	1633	Separate the 2 dates with a dash, no spaces between Include all 4 digits for both years
One of 2 years (work was done in either 1631 or 1633)	1631 or 1633	1631	1633	Use the word 'or'. Include all 4 digits for both years
Range of dates (work was done sometime between 1745 and 1748)	1745/1748	1745	1748	Separate the 2 dates with a slash, with no spaces between Include all 4 digits for both years
Decades	1930s early 1930s late 1930s	1930 1930 1935	1939 1934 1939	no apostrophe before 's' 'early' and 'late' all in lower case
Circa	c.1900 c.1600 or 1610 c.1510-1520 c.1510-c.1520	1895 1595 1505 1505	1905 1610 1520 1525	Use c. Don't use 'about', 'circa', 'ca' or 'c' No space between c. and date
Before	1686-before 1770 before 1686-1750	1686 no begin date	1770 1750	Use 'before' Don't use 'prior to'
After	1823-after 1941 after 1822-1900	1823 1822	no end date 1900	Use 'after' Don't use 'post'
Uncertainty	?1750	1750	1750	Place a question mark before the doubtful element without a space. Do not use 'probably'
More precise dates	November 1900 21 January 1890	1900 1890	1900 1890	 Dates given in full should be entered as day month year without punctuation or ordinal abbreviation such as rd, th, nd

Table 3: Data Entry Conventions when entering Object Dates and Search Dates into TMS (excerpt).

Author Index